MW01503130

Endorsements for Forward Sioux Falls

Since its inception in 1987, Forward Sioux Falls economic development program initiatives have spanned more than thirty years of success for the Sioux Falls community, area, and region. The Joint Venture Forward Sioux Falls program of the Greater Sioux Falls Chamber of Commerce and the Sioux Falls Development Foundation has succeeded in helping achieve record levels of attracting and retaining high quality jobs, capital investment, technology development, workforce and educational development, issues advocacy, and "game changing" quality-of-life projects. More importantly, Forward Sioux Falls has created a culture of leadership, collaboration, aspiration and success through generations of leaders public and private in the Sioux Falls area.

—Evan Nolte
Retired President and CEO of the
Sioux Falls Area Chamber of Commerce

I believe the Forward Sioux Falls program has defined the "modern era" of Sioux Falls since it began in 1987. The community leaders of that day developed a vision and an economic development platform that have changed the trajectory of our community and the Sioux Falls region forever. Together, we've achieved new heights well beyond what anyone could have envisioned because community leaders ever since continue to carry the torch.

Community leaders in Sioux Falls long ago recognized that economic development is a team sport. Forward Sioux Falls continues to bring our community together around a common set of priorities, pooling our time, talent, and treasure to address challenges and maximize opportunities. This has truly set Sioux Falls apart. It's now up to us to carry on.

—Dave Rozenboom
President, First PREMIER Bank

This book is a salute to the hundreds of leaders and staff who have been dedicated to carrying out the shared vision of Forward Sioux Falls. We all believe that our commitment to this effort has made, and will continue to make Sioux Falls a better community to live and work.

—Mary Medema
Retired Director of Workforce Development
Sioux Falls Development Foundation/Forward Sioux Falls (1998-2016)

Forward Sioux Falls does exactly as the name says. It is the strategy and funding that helps launch Sioux Falls Forward. Our community leaders know we cannot just sit back and hope growth happens. We need to continue to take action to be a progressive region and Forward Sioux Falls allows us to do this!

—Pam Hanneman
VP Business Banking Manager, First PREMIER Bank

It's important and useful to understand a community's history and the events and people who shaped it. This book entertainingly tells of a pivotal period in the life of Sioux Falls that shows that its current enviable position didn't just happen by accident or good fortune. An encouraging and fascinating look behind the scenes of 'city building' that will instruct as well as inspire.

—Howard Benson
Founder, National Community Development Services

Dependable and steadfast, Forward Sioux Falls continues to strengthen the economy of our community by providing allocated dollars to areas most needed. This public/private partnership shows the commitment businesses have to Sioux Falls and its sustained growth. With continued support for Forward Sioux Falls, we are paving the way for generations to come.

—Lucas J. Fiegen
AIA; Vice President, Fiegen Construction Co.

Many of the initiatives funded by Forward Sioux Falls are so ingrained into the fabric of Sioux Falls and its business community that most citizens don't even realize Forward Sioux Falls was a catalyst in their creation. Forward Sioux Falls doesn't just support quality of life projects and business attraction, it is also vital to workforce development, innovation, entrepreneurship, international trade, and governmental advocacy, among other things. Sioux Falls would not be the community it is without Forward Sioux Falls.

—Dan Doyle
Partner, Cutler Law Firm, LLP
2020-21 Chamber Board Chairman

Sioux Falls has become the envy of many communities aspiring to achieve long-term economic growth and prosperity, thanks in large part to the work of Forward Sioux Falls. Many of them have tried to emulate the Forward Sioux Falls model, but the intense and sustained commitment of Sioux Falls' very top business and community leaders is what distinguishes this organization—and this community—from so many others.

—Tom DiFiore
President, National Community Development Services

For more than 30 years, Sioux Falls visionaries have banded together to attract businesses and create jobs in their home community through Forward Sioux Falls. A unique joint venture between the Chamber of Commerce and the Development Foundation, Forward Sioux Falls has been integral to the continued growth and quality of life in this city.

—Dennis Daugaard
Former Governor of South Dakota

I think the name "Forward Sioux Falls" speaks volumes to what the program has meant not only to Sioux Falls, but also to the State of South Dakota. For over three decades, Forward Sioux Falls has been Sioux Falls' "engine for growth" and a "catalyst" for positive thinking within the business community.

—Tony Bour
Chairman, Showplace Wood Products, Inc.

For more than four decades, Forward Sioux Falls has been the foundation on which the unprecedented success of our community has been built. Public, private, large and small businesses, as well as individuals have come together to promote and grow the qualities of Sioux Falls.

—Dana Dykhouse
CEO, First PREMIER Bank

Without Forward Sioux Falls, Sioux Falls wouldn't be what it is today. A growing, dynamic, thriving community that affords the opportunity for great quality of life.

—Jim Schmidt
President, Sioux Empire Housing Partnership
and Lincoln County Commissioner

The results of Forward Sioux Falls since its formation in 1987 can be seen across the community. Through this community development program, we have worked together to diversify and strengthen our economy, enhancing economic development and quality of life for people across the Sioux Falls area. It's a collaboration that is the envy of our peer communities, laying a strong foundation for economic growth that has positioned us well for the future. I look forward to seeing the results and success we will continue to achieve together!

—Paul TenHaken
Mayor, City of Sioux Falls

Forward Sioux Falls has been and continues to be the economic catalyst of our fine city. Forward Sioux Falls initially moved our community out of a negative posture into a very positive and active force for economic growth and stability. Prior to Forward Sioux Falls, many fine projects did not become a reality without multiple votes for approval by the electorate (i.e., the arena and Lincoln High School). Today, new and progressive projects are received with enthusiasm and total community support. Thanks to the Greater Sioux Falls Chamber of Commerce and the Sioux Falls Development Foundation for their leadership and vision in the creation of Forward Sioux Falls.

—Lyle Schroeder
Retired CEO of Sioux Valley Hospital

FORWARD
SIOUX FALLS

FORWARD
SIOUX FALLS

ADVANCING OUR REGION'S ECONOMY THROUGH
VISION, STRATEGY, AND COLLABORATION

THRONE
PUBLISHING GROUP

Publisher: Throne Publishing Group and StoryWay
Editor: Elizabeth Duffy, Certified StoryWay Guide
Editor: Marguerite Bonnett, Certified StoryWay Guide
Editor: Tracy Jenkens, Certified StoryWay Guide
Designer: Tim Murray
Writer: Dirk Lammers

Text is set in 11/14 Quadraat OT and Proxima Nova

For bulk orders, signed copies, or for a Forward Sioux Falls team member to speak at your
future event, please contact:

Forward Sioux Falls
200 N. Phillips Ave, Suite #200
Sioux Falls, SD 57104
605.373.2008

We are proud and honored to be a part of the Sioux Falls region. In our attempt to diligently portray a few of the many stories and people that have contributed to the nationally acclaimed economic growth of our city, it would have taken volumes of books to mention every story and every leader who has played a role. We thank you for your involvement and we look forward to writing the next chapters with you.

Contents

KEY OUTCOMES

Since its inception in 1987, Forward Sioux Falls has been a key driver to transform the Sioux Falls region, leading to these remarkable results:

Job Growth

236% Growth Since 1987
91,000 Net New Jobs

 **Best Small Place for Business and Careers**
12 of the last 20 years

 **City in the US for Young Professionals**
according to SmartAsset

Population Growth

214% Growth Since 1987

142,200 Net New Residents

PRESENT

1987

1856

#7 Top 100 Places to Live
according to Livability

#10 Best City for Entrepreneurs
according to FitSmallBusiness

FORWARD
SIOUX FALLS

CHAPTER 1

Unlocking Our Potential

A STROLL TODAY ALONG DOWNTOWN Sioux Falls' Phillips Avenue reveals crowds of residents and visitors frequenting lively restaurants, coffee shops, retail stores, and boutiques. The street serves as a gateway to the city's crown jewel, Falls Park, which offers breathtaking views of water cascading across spectacular rose-colored quartzite formations from numerous paved paths or the five-story observation tower.

Sioux Falls, South Dakota, has emerged into a vibrant Upper Midwest city at the crossroads of Interstates 29 and 90, growing over the last half-century into a dynamic metropolitan area of more than a quarter-million residents. Sioux Falls' economy, which has always shown strength in retail, wholesale, trade, and agriculture, has diversified into financial services, healthcare, and biotechnology, and its transformation has opened eyes from coast to coast. Sioux Falls has been named Forbes' Best Small City for Business and Careers for an amazing 12 out of 20 years[1] and has recently been named as SmartAsset's Best U.S. City for Young Professionals, among numerous other honors.[2] The city's safe and clean neighborhoods, robust public schools, bustling regional airport, and

[1] Horan, Stephanie, "The Best Cities for Young Professionals – 2019 Edition," *SmartAsset*, July 10, 2020, accessed July 16, 2020, https://smartasset.com/mortgage/best-cities-for-young-professionals-2019

[2] "The Best Small Places For Businesses And Careers," *Forbes*, accessed July 16, 2020, https://www.forbes.com/best-places-for-business/list/small/

29-mile bike trail landed it on Livability.com's lists of Best Places to Live and Best Cities for Entrepreneurs.[3]

Sioux Falls wasn't always on the national radar for such accolades.

Just four decades earlier, the metropolitan area entered the 1980s with a population of about 110,000, marking consecutive decades of steady yet unspectacular growth. John Morrell & Co. served as Sioux Falls' single largest employer, and residents fortunate enough to hold full-time jobs at the meatpacking plant expressed great pride in those positions. The plant contributed greatly to the community and its presence significantly boosted the economy, but the mere threat of a worker strike or round of layoffs served as a reminder of the need to further diversify beyond the agricultural economy.

IT WAS ABOUT THAT TIME that Evan Nolte arrived in town to interview for the position of Executive Vice President with the Sioux Falls Area Chamber of Commerce. He recalls a volunteer leader taking him on a guided tour highlighting points of community pride—charming residential neighborhoods, growing hospitals, and the thriving 41st Street retail corridor. The itinerary basically skipped downtown Sioux Falls, and that was likely not an accident.

"It was almost like it was conspicuously avoided," said Nolte, who led the Chamber from 1979 through 2017.

Like many US cities, Sioux Falls got caught up in the nationwide urban renewal movement in the '60s and '70s that led to the destruction of many once-iconic buildings. An ill-advised decision to turn several blocks of Phillips Avenue into a pedestrian mall furthered the demise, thinning downtown's few remaining retail offerings. Falls Park of the early '80s was "basically just a mess," with garbage gathering in ditches, limited parking, no obvious entrance route, and no real walkways surrounding the waterfalls.

3 "2016 Best Cities For Entrepreneurs," *Livability*, accessed July 16, 2020, https://livability.com/list/best-cities-for-entrepreneurs/2016/10?page=2.

"I wouldn't have recommended anyone go down there at night," Nolte said.

The city simply wasn't thriving as it stood caught in a conflict between business leaders who felt Sioux Falls could prosper and a group of people "living in yesterday and wanting tomorrow to be like yesterday," said Lyle Schroeder, then president of Sioux Valley Hospital.

Key business leaders envisioned a city with bigger and better things on the horizon. Sioux Falls boasted a modern regional airport, a growing public zoo, a quality K-12 school system, and several higher-learning institutions. The Sioux Falls Development Foundation built industrial parks to draw manufacturing and wholesale tenants, and city leaders worked with the federal government to establish the EROS Data Center, a Landsat satellite imaging facility on farmland north of the city. The 41st Street retail corridor, anchored by the Western Mall and the larger and newer Empire Mall, regularly drew shoppers from a three-state region.

KEY BUSINESS LEADERS ENVISIONED A CITY WITH BIGGER AND BETTER THINGS ON THE HORIZON.

But still, there was an opportunity to strengthen the city through the diversification of its economy. Sioux Falls found the opportunity to begin tackling those goals through a 1980 effort spearheaded by then South Dakota Governor Bill Janklow. The colorful leader convinced South Dakota legislators, with the support of the state's banking community, to pass two laws to entice Citibank to relocate its credit card operations from New York. One lifted the cap on card interest rates while the other allowed out-of-state bank holding companies to create South Dakota subsidiaries. Citibank South Dakota launched in Sioux Falls in February 1981, initially managing three million credit card accounts from three rented floors of downtown office space.

Within years, Citibank South Dakota moved into a new sprawling complex and challenged John Morrell as the city's largest employer. The groundbreaking legislation enticed other financial services companies to come to Sioux Falls. The burgeoning financial services industry "opened our eyes to the opportunity in the larger world," said longtime Sioux Falls attorney Doug Hajek, and it spurred subsidiary growth in such sectors as office furniture and computer services.

"It wasn't just their own direct employees," Hajek said. "There were a lot of adjacent industries which basically either sprung up or greatly expanded because of Citibank's move here."

Sioux Falls was gaining momentum in its economic development efforts, but several missing pieces remained. Newcomers such as former Caterpillar Inc. executive Charlie Kearns and Citibank's new leaders joined some existing voices in bemoaning the city's lack of cultural and performing arts amenities. Kearns, to whom Nolte referred as a "positive rabble-rouser," relocated from Peoria, Illinois, to open machinery dealer franchises in Sioux Falls and Rapid City. He and Citibank's Dick McCrossen and Charlie Long became friends and brainstormed ways to advance economic development even further.

Community leaders dared to ask, could Sioux Falls replicate the Citibank formula by enticing other companies and industries? Could Sioux Falls compete with larger Midwest communities like Des Moines, Omaha, Lincoln, and even Minneapolis? And could it win on a national scale?

Community and corporate confidence continued percolating as Sioux Falls scored a high-profile breakthrough on a public-sector project. The Sioux Falls Downtown Development Corporation rebuilt a city block at Phillips Avenue and 9th Street, providing multi-story office space for Western Surety Co. and other tenants. City leaders began reopening parts of the failed Phillips Avenue Pedestrian Mall to vehicle traffic, and retailers slowly returned. In light of all this success, what else could go downtown?

A coalition of organizations and individuals led by the Sioux Falls Downtown Development Corporation lobbied to build a $30 million convention center, performing arts center,

SIOUX FALLS WAS GAINING MOMENTUM IN ITS ECONOMIC DEVELOPMENT EFFORTS, BUT SEVERAL MISSING PIECES REMAINED.

and hotel in downtown Sioux Falls. The project would draw top business conventions, theater, and musical events to the city, provide tourists with a place to stay, and boost the community's tax base. It seemed like a win for everyone, but the proposal faced strong opposition from the Taxpayers Against the Convention Center Obligation (TACCO) committee, a grassroots group founded by local broadcaster and humorist E.C. "Red" Stangland. (Stangland, by the way, popularized those "Ole and Lena" jokes commonly prompting chuckles and eyerolls across the Upper Midwest.)

TACCO members argued that the city shouldn't take on future obligations by issuing bonds to fund new projects, and they appealed to the anti-growth sentiment that feared heavier traffic, higher crime, and general change. Many of Sioux Falls' forward-thinking business leaders disagreed with TACCO, but voters rejected the project by a 52 percent to 48 percent margin. The stinging defeat delivered a powerful wake-up call.[4] If pro-growth advocates wanted to galvanize the community and push Sioux Falls into the next century, they'd have to work together and organize more effectively.

"It was very, very disheartening and disappointing, but it further fueled the fire," Nolte said.

Community leaders recognized that they were going to have to build a strong coalition to advance future economic development projects. They needed a bold visionary to guide them on that journey, and they found that person in Howard Benson, an Atlanta-based consultant who founded National Community Development Services (NCDS). Benson had established the widely successful Forward Atlanta program before branching off on his own to assist Forward Metro Denver and other communities with their economic development initiatives.

Nolte called Benson, and the two talked about Sioux Falls' need to spur development, create new jobs, recruit new businesses, design professional marketing materials, and promote

4 Cunningham, Doug. "Voters say no: City scraps downtown development plan." *Argus Leader*, August 14, 1985, accessed July 16, 2020 via Newspapers.com.

the city's growing healthcare facilities across the region. Benson advised Nolte to take a broad look at the various issues.

"I suggested that rather than piecemeal efforts in all these things, there needed to be a central focus for those efforts with enough time and resources behind them to make a real impact," Benson said.

Nolte set up an early morning meeting at the Chamber's 10th Street office, inviting Benson to address more than a dozen forward-thinking business leaders, including representatives of the Chamber and Development Foundation. The executives, who represented financial services, healthcare, retail, manufacturing, and media, included Lyle Schroeder, Charlie Kearns, Dick McCrossen, Lewis Drug President Mark Griffin, KELO-TV Owner Joe Floyd and President Evans Nord, and First Bank President David Birkeland. The group selected Schroeder to chair the meeting, even though he hadn't envisioned himself ever holding the gavel.

"Lyle was one of those leaders who would make a phone call, and people would be there," Nolte said.

Schroeder ran Sioux Valley Hospital, one of the community's largest health care facilities, and had been active in numerous community organizations, but he hadn't yet taken a leadership role within those community organizations. The group assured him he had the talent and ability to make great things happen, and he proved them right. It's a story that has repeated itself time and time again over Forward Sioux Falls' long history; strong servants who initially don't see themselves as leaders step up, lead with strength and humility, and flourish.

Benson quickly surmised that the group was eager to embrace new ideas, and he sensed no skepticism or doubt. He described Sioux Falls as a nice, medium-sized city that was a far better community than anyone outside the area realized. Though it lacked a critical mass to drive such next-level building blocks as arts and culture, it offered plenty of benefits to promote.

Benson then passed out examples of marketing brochures showing how other cities hyped their amenities. Sioux Falls had nothing comparable, as neither the Sioux Falls Area Chamber of Commerce nor the Sioux Falls Development Foundation devoted significant resources to marketing.

"If you don't project an image," Benson told the group, "then the world is going to put one on you." Sioux Falls wasn't telling and selling its story to the outside world, so how could it expect anyone to take notice?

"Sioux Falls didn't make the short list. It wasn't even on the list," Benson said bluntly. "It just wasn't on anybody's radar."

The city had the essentials to go to market, Benson said, but if it wanted to reach the next level, it needed to aggressively target business location planners, meeting planners, potential employees, and vacationers. The meeting attendees nodded in agreement.

"We knew that we weren't matching up with some of the aggressive communities around the country," Schroeder said. "And we knew those that were out there doing their marketing and telling their story were accomplishing things that we were not at the time."

The community was at a crossroads, and the status quo was no longer enough.

"What we were talking about made good sense, and if we were going to be a competitor in the world as we would go forward, we had to do those things," Schroeder said.

The city was ready for a push, and that push was going to come from the business sector. The group of leaders left the meeting room with a resolve to win and a mission to ensure that people across the country would know the name "Sioux Falls."

"SIOUX FALLS DIDN'T MAKE THE SHORT LIST. IT WASN'T EVEN ON THE LIST."

CHAPTER 2

The Resolve to Win

COMMUNITY LEADERS LEFT the Howard Benson meeting with confidence about the city's future and a renewed sense of urgency.

If Sioux Falls wanted to raise its profile to compete with larger Midwestern counterparts, its leaders needed to adopt a bold approach and take some risks. The community required a comprehensive economic development plan customized to its opportunities and challenges. Business leaders focused their goals on diversifying the city's economy, creating more jobs, and—most importantly—marketing the city into regional and national prominence.

Benson worked with the Chamber's Evan Nolte and Roger Hainje, a senior staffer at the Development Foundation, to sketch out details of a strategic initiative approach that had scored significant gains in Denver and Atlanta. But compared to Colorado's largest city and Georgia's largest city, South Dakota's largest city was far more remote with far fewer residents. Could such an approach transform Sioux Falls?

During an after-hours meeting at the downtown Holiday Inn, Benson helped Nolte and Hainje devise a plan to organize and fund a four-year economic development initiative that would evolve into Forward Sioux Falls. Though the cocktail napkin holding etchings of the program's origins is long gone, Forward Sioux Falls' impact continues to resonate. Benson said he was impressed with the two energetic young men who, unlike most he had met in similar capacities, showed no inkling of "turf protection" or competitiveness.

"While each had to contend with scarcity of resources and keeping their respective supporters aware of their organization's value, their focus was on how they could mutually help create sustainable growth and improve the quality of life in the region," Benson said.

SIOUX FALLS NEEDED TO DO SOMETHING IT HAD NEVER DONE BEFORE.

Sioux Falls needed to do something it had never done before—sell itself nationally. That would require a well-funded marketing campaign, but who was best suited to lead such an effort? The Chamber primarily focused on advocating for area businesses, though it did promote tourism and conventions through its Convention and Visitors Bureau (CVB). The Chamber's total marketing budget the previous year was just under $75,000. The Development Foundation promoted business and industrial economic development, but it traditionally focused on land development and devoted less than $20,000 a year to marketing.

If the Chamber were solely tasked with marketing Sioux Falls, its directors probably would have said it was work the Development Foundation should be doing. If the Development Foundation's directors were asked to take charge, they probably would have wondered if it was more of a Chamber role. It became clear that any comprehensive economic development/marketing effort should involve a coming together of both organizations, said Lyle Schroeder, president of Sioux Valley Hospital.

"By joining the two, you really had the community together," Schroeder said.

With a basic framework in place, the Chamber and Development Foundation brought Benson back to Sioux Falls to present the strategic initiative concept to the organizations' boards. Benson made his pitch during a luncheon meeting at the Minnehaha Country Club and fielded questions before each board sequestered into separate meeting rooms to debate and vote on the proposal. The boards approved resolutions to jointly hire Benson and National Community Development Services (NCDS) to build a case statement, and the seed planted in that initial meeting began sprouting into Forward Sioux Falls.

Benson got to work expanding his efforts into a detailed feasibility study, spending weeks gathering input from hundreds of community leaders on what they needed to do today to ensure the vitality of tomorrow.

"The direction was, let's find out what people are thinking, what they might support, show them what we could do to get to be a competitive city, put some price tags on it," Nolte said.

Nolte noted the importance of involving so many stakeholders early in the process, as businesses and corporations typically don't financially support things that do not fit into their mission. "And when a community of businesses puts aside individual goals and joins together to advance a shared mission," Benson added, "they ensure the health and sustainability of their community."

Corporate leaders need to be "involved, prominent, and maybe even dominant" in moving their community forward. Elected officials by nature come and go and political winds constantly blow, but businesses have a vested interest in the health and sustainability of their community and must stay laser-focused on success, Benson said.

"If they're simply bystanders, if they're takers and not contributors to the economic sustainability and viability of the community, then you're sunk," he said. "They're constantly being wooed and offered deals to pick up and relocate or combine their operations. So, having business at the table and involved

"WHEN A COMMUNITY OF BUSINESSES PUTS ASIDE INDIVIDUAL GOALS AND JOINS TOGETHER TO ADVANCE A SHARED MISSION, THEY ENSURE THE HEALTH AND SUSTAINABILITY OF THEIR COMMUNITY."

and engaged makes absolute sense."

Once the Chamber and Development Foundation boards reviewed the feasibility study, suggested changes, and approved the plan, Forward Sioux Falls was nearly ready to move forward. One pressing question remained: How were the boards going to manage the program? Everyone agreed that both the Chamber and the Development Foundation should participate, but how should such a collaboration be formally structured? Should Forward Sioux Falls be established as a new, distinct organization? Should one organization take the lead while the other offered support?

Nolte and Hainje, who had just been promoted to lead the Development Foundation, sought help from attorney Russ Greenfield, the Development Foundation's legal counsel. During a meeting in a small Boyce Law Firm conference room, Greenfield suggested structuring the program as a joint venture rather than a partnership, and he drafted a four-page agreement to be presented to both boards. The fact that the document could be so short demonstrated the mutual respect each organization had for the other, Nolte said.

"You don't do something like that unless there's a lot of trust," he said. "That document was very basic."

The agreement put Forward Sioux Falls under the leadership of a Joint Venture Management Committee (JVMC) that included the five executive committee members from the Chamber board, the five executive committee members from the Development Foundation board, and additional appointed business leaders from the community. Officials introduced Forward Sioux Falls to the public on April 1, 1987, setting a fundraising goal of $1.4 million.

Forward Sioux Falls' most innovative endeavor, compared to previous economic development efforts, was setting aside $640,000—more than 45 percent of the program goal—over four years for a coordinated marketing campaign. That figure was a

OFFICIALS INTRODUCED FORWARD SIOUX FALLS TO THE PUBLIC ON APRIL 1, 1987, SETTING A FUNDRAISING GOAL OF $1.4 MILLION.

huge jump from monies previously allocated by the Chamber and Development Foundation, and it indicated a newfound resolve to make Sioux Falls known.

The marketing initiative included research to identify growing companies that could be invited to Sioux Falls, followed by national and regional advertising efforts to demonstrate that Sioux Falls is a great place to move their businesses. Another $150,000 was set aside to produce high-quality promotional materials to showcase the city's business-friendly attributes.

Most community members applauded the lofty goals, but some thought they were an overreach.

"They were incremental in their vision," Benson said of the naysayers. "They were not bold; they were not as aggressive. As one of my friends out there told me one time, 'Well, if you've never seen a cow, a calf is a big animal.'"

Another challenge resurfaced later in 1987 after city commissioners proposed financing a $2.8 million parking ramp and bus transfer facility to be built along First Avenue between 10th and 11th streets. TACCO, now retooled as the Taxpayers Action by Concerned Citizens Organization, gathered nearly 2,000 signatures to force a public vote on the project, assuming the majority of Sioux Falls residents would vote against growth.

Investment executive Gene McGowan declared he had enough. He teamed up with several business leaders to launch a broad-based advocacy group called Citizens for Progress, meeting nearly every day to promote the project, share information, and garner public support. The Argus Leader declared in an editorial that the parking ramp vote was, to an extent, a referendum on downtown growth.

"The election will measure the city's confidence in itself," the newspaper declared.[1]

Voters on June 16, 1987, approved the financing package by a 58 percent to 42 percent margin, and TACCO's power began to wane. With the wheels set in motion on a significant public

[1] "Voters should say yes to new parking ramp." *Argus Leader*, June 12, 1987, accessed July 16, 2020 via Newspapers.com.

project, Forward Sioux Falls leaders continued raising money for their economic development effort.[2]

Schroeder, who was selected to chair Forward Sioux Falls, said the city was ready for a push, and corporate leaders were actively responding to the call.

"They cared about the city, and they were willing to dig in their corporate pockets, and some individual pockets, in order to make something like this happen," he said.

The goals set in the program made good sense, Schroeder said, and if Sioux Falls was going to be a competitor in the world, the city would have to take such steps. As a promise to its investors, Forward Sioux Falls provided measurable objectives.

Attaching metrics to goals is an important part of the Forward Sioux Falls program's repeated success, Nolte said.

"If companies are going to set aside money to support something, they want to see a return on their investment," he said.

The team was confident in its approach and was building momentum. Forward Sioux Falls was finally in operation and picking up steam. A great future was on the horizon.

[2] Erpenbach, Steve. "Parking ramp issue passes." *Argus Leader*, June 17, 1987, accessed July 16, 2020 via Newspapers.com.

CHAPTER 3

How We Make Decisions

WHEN SIOUX FALLS BUSINESS LEADERS created the first Forward Sioux Falls initiative in 1987 to boost the city's economic development, they likely had no idea they'd be creating a model that would pay dividends time and time again.

Sioux Falls' decades of achievements and accomplishments have not happened by chance. They are the result of a highly intentional process, and it's important to take a step back and detail the model that has led to, and continues to lead to, success.

Forward Sioux Falls' process brings together the city's business leaders in a collaborative way to identify opportunities and challenges, and it has proven resilient and successful. Every Forward Sioux Falls program has met or surpassed its fundraising goal, addressed pressing needs, and delivered results.

Although the first four editions spanned four years, each of the next three Forward Sioux Falls programs have spanned five years. Each begins with a discovery phase, transitions into a campaign phase, and advances into an action phase.

Why five years? Leaders serving on the Joint Venture Management Committee (JVMC) that guides the programs have found that by only having to devote time to raising funds once every five years, they can spend the majority of time and effort on getting work done. Sure, specific goals may advance during a five-year span, but the main pillars of the program stand firm—that Forward Sioux Falls is, at its core, an economic development program, so each committee starts with and builds upon the current program of work.

"We understand this is part of a longer-term effort," said First PREMIER Bank President Dave Rozenboom, who co-chaired the Forward Sioux Falls VII campaign and subsequently served as JVMC chair during the program's implementation. "We're just taking the baton and running the next leg of the race."

Business recruitment serves as the centerpiece of economic development, so every Forward Sioux Falls program involves efforts to spur business retention and expansion. International trade and expansion of air service are also common themes, as they help ensure a vibrant, well-connected community. Other common aspects addressed by Forward Sioux Falls include workforce development, entrepreneurship, innovation, advocacy, and quality-of-life initiatives.

Conversations about specific program objectives typically begin about 18 months before campaign kickoff with a discovery phase conducted by the JVMC. Rozenboom says committee members are extremely informed community leaders who are plugged into Sioux Falls.

"When we convene, we've got a finger on the pulse of what's happening on the economic front," he said.

By summer in the year before launch, the campaign enters a quiet phase in which consultants from National Community Development Services (NCDS) conduct confidential one-on-one interviews with more than 50 top potential investors, many of whom contribute each cycle. NCDS lists seven fundamental elements of a successful fundraising campaign:
• Compelling need
• Effective plan to meet the need

- Board/staff/inner circle fundraising strength
- Positive board/staff/inner circle public image
- Constituency has adequate financial resources
- Potential campaign leaders available, interested, and committed
- Sense of urgency should exist

In addition to summarizing the previous Forward Sioux Falls programs and sharing the proposed objectives of the new program, NCDS consultants ask for honest feedback about the objectives and question whether anything should be modified, added, or taken away. They also gauge investors' potential commitment to the campaign.

The honest feedback is welcomed because the committee wants to reach consensus and set a realistic fundraising goal. The conversations provide a litmus test for the rest of the campaign, Rozenboom said.

"This allows us as a community to pool our time, talent, and treasure on a common set of priorities with the goal of economic development," he said. "Everybody's got a chance to weigh in."

NCDS then compiles all the feedback into a report with recommendations for the JVMC's review. CEO Howard Benson said community needs drive the program content, and the program content should drive the funding requirement. This commitment helps build trust.

"If the community needs are huge, then you may need huge resources. If they are not, then you may not need as much money," Benson said. "You never want to say, 'Let's raise all we can and we'll spend all we get.'"

Once the committee finalizes the objectives and sets the fundraising goal, the program advances to the campaign phase to begin raising the money needed to carry out the body of work. The outreach begins with the core, expands to Sioux Falls' other large firms, and then reaches out to medium- to small-sized businesses. The campaign then goes public during the

"EVERYBODY'S GOT A CHANCE TO WEIGH IN."

November before launch as the committee tries to widen the program's base.

Retired Avera Health Chief Operating Officer Fred Slunecka, who worked on Forward Sioux Falls II, III, and IV, said it's important to emerge from the planning process with a common vision to overcome any competitive instincts and issues that might arise.

"There's a very strong commitment by all the players that once an agenda is established, then that is the agenda," Slunecka said. The vision and strategy are backed by the leaders, and everyone focuses on accomplishing the set goals.

IT'S IMPORTANT TO EMERGE FROM THE PLANNING PROCESS WITH A COMMON VISION.

With the fundraising complete, the Joint Venture Management Committee then assigns either the Chamber or the Development Foundation to carry out the assigned work and allocates money to achieve each goal.

"Everyone knows their part of the task," Rozenboom said.

Although Forward Sioux Falls programs work on a five-year plan, annual budgets are approved to ensure accountability and provide the flexibility to adapt to changing times.

For instance, when Forward Sioux Falls VI launched, the nation was coming out of the Great Recession with a national unemployment rate nearing 10 percent. Everyone was trying to create jobs, and although Sioux Falls' unemployment rate was far lower than the nation's, the issue was front and center. But as the nation emerged from recession and unemployment dropped, it quickly became clear in Sioux Falls that creating jobs was not going to be the problem; the problem was going to be filling jobs. Workforce development became the new buzzword, and the flexibility to adapt was key.

Oftentimes, initiatives created by Forward Sioux Falls break off into self-sustaining programs. The Sioux Falls Sports Authority, which attracts international, national, regional, and state sporting events to the area, was born in 2006 out of Forward Sioux Falls IV.[1] The Chamber's Young Professionals Network

[1] Swenson, Rob. "Sioux Falls Sports Authority to define function: Board may attract events, improve facilities." *Argus Leader*, November 15, 2006, accessed July 16, 2020 via Newspapers.com.

(YPN) program started with Forward Sioux Falls V. Its work has helped earn the city recognition from SmartAsset as one of the Best Cities for Young Professionals for three consecutive years.[2]

Because Forward Sioux Falls prides itself on being a good steward of investors' funds, transparency and communication are key. The JVMC meets regularly to review the progress of initiatives and take action on relevant items. Ongoing communication with investors includes distribution of an online newsletter, face-to-face visits, and investor briefings. Annual audits verify that pledges and investments are handled correctly.

Near the end of each program, the committee commissions an economic impact study for each industry sector. These studies have shown that there is a quantifiable return for every dollar invested. And because investors see the value, they can encourage others to contribute to the next campaign.

"We are all investing in Sioux Falls," Rozenboom said. "There's a positive return, and we've been able to demonstrate that."

Forward Sioux Falls' highly intentional process ensures business leaders that their investments will help the city address its opportunities and challenges and deliver results. And each time a program delivers, it encourages additional leaders to join in the next effort.

[2] Horan, Stephanie, , "The Best Cities for Young Professionals – 2019 Edition," SmartAsset, July 10, 2020, accessed July 16, 2020, https://smartasset.com/mortgage/best-cities-for-young-professionals-2019

CHAPTER 4

A Bold Vision

SIOUX FALLS BUSINESS LEADERS embarked on the inaugural
Forward Sioux Falls program with the confidence that the city
could be more effective if its leaders combined their time, talent,
and treasure around a common set of priorities.

To narrow those priorities into actionable tasks, the
Chamber's Evan Nolte, the Development Foundation's Roger
Hainje, and consultant Howard Benson diligently prepared a
detailed needs assessment. The trio set up numerous meetings
to seek honest feedback from business leaders and quickly
learned how heavily Sioux Falls was graced with a wealth of energetic business leaders who were willing, and even anxious, to do
something to make a difference. These leaders weren't satisfied
with Sioux Falls' current rate of growth, and they expressed a
strong desire for the Chamber and the Development Foundation
to work together to move the city forward.

"People wanted change," Benson said. "They didn't want to
remain where they were."

And, most importantly, they wanted Forward Sioux Falls to
spread the word about the city's amenities and advantages. Sioux
Falls had a strong business and tax climate and a favorable cost

"PEOPLE WANTED CHANGE. THEY DIDN'T WANT TO REMAIN WHERE THEY WERE."

of living. It was a safe, family-friendly community that offered such quality-of-life benefits as superior schools, peaceful parks, and robust retail. Sioux Falls had the goods, but it needed to upgrade its marketing materials to communicate such benefits across the nation.

Nolte said the city at the time didn't even have a good community brochure to distribute, and the examples Benson shared from other communities wowed the group and convinced them of a professional marketing campaign's potential.

"Some of these materials just made your mouth water," Nolte said. "And at the time we didn't have the funds in either organization to be able to pay for that."

"THAT WAS A BIG BITE FOR A NEW IDEA, BUT THE COMMUNITY LEADERSHIP RESPONDED ENTHUSIASTICALLY."

Forward Sioux Falls prioritized marketing the city in its program objectives, but it also vowed to tackle more traditional business recruitment and retention targets such as:

- Improve, expand, and diversify the economy of South Dakota and Sioux Falls
- Attract expansion and relocation of firms which can benefit Sioux Falls area assets
- Increase employment opportunities and generate additional payroll for area citizens
- Expand the tax base of local governments by increasing capital investment in the Sioux Falls area
- Continue the dominance of Sioux Falls as a medical and retail center
- Increase job retention activities supporting existing industry and assist in the creation of new business

The stakes were high, as the community leaders being asked to invest in Forward Sioux Falls were going to want to see results. Committee members responded by setting measurable goals that were as bold as the objectives:

- Increase employment in the Sioux Falls area by 6,000 additional jobs, accelerating the present growth rate by 50 percent

- Generate $90 million in new payroll for area citizens
- Attract capital investment totaling $105 million
- Increase awareness of Sioux Falls by 20 percent among national/regional corporate decision makers and opinion leaders

It was clear that such efforts would take a significant sum of money, but it was important that Forward Sioux Falls not over-reach in setting its fundraising goal. The committee settled on a bold yet attainable number of $1.4 million.

"That was a big bite for a new idea," said First PREMIER Bank President Dave Rozenboom. "But the community leadership responded enthusiastically."

The campaign committee surmised that it had buy-in from the community's large businesses, as many of those business leaders had contributed their thoughts—and their financial commitment—during the needs-assessment process. But if the program was to grow into a community-wide economic development effort, it would have to embrace inclusivity and draw support from small- to medium-sized businesses.

Forward Sioux Falls Campaign Chairman Lyle Schroeder tasked fellow Sioux Valley Hospital executive Dick Bohy to find someone to lead investor recruitment for the small- to medium-sized business sector. Bohy, in turn, made a call to Pam Hanneman, a 28-year-old manager running the Midco Communications call center on Phillips Avenue.

Hanneman knew Bohy through the Chamber and United Way, but she initially had no idea why Bohy and Schroeder invited her to lunch at the Westward Ho Country Club that day. As they sat near a window overlooking Westward Ho's golf course, the pair talked about how Forward Sioux Falls was looking to boost economic development by attracting businesses to the community, encouraging existing businesses to expand and create new jobs, diversifying the economy, and marketing the city across the country. Then Bohy and Schroeder got to the point: they wanted her to lead that sector of the campaign.

Bohy described Hanneman as an energetic and positive up-and-coming community leader who eagerly stepped into an unknown role and took charge.

"She exuded capability," Bohy said. "Anything she did, she did well."

Hanneman said she was unsure of exactly what the role would entail, and she's not sure that Bohy and Schroeder knew either, but she knew the program was crucial for the community and felt confident she'd have the support of leadership.

"I said I would do it," said Hanneman, who later became the vice president of business banking for First PREMIER Bank. "I'm always up for a challenge."

Hanneman quickly realized that she was taking on an overwhelming mission, as the committee wanted to reach hundreds of businesses within a concentrated campaign. How would they set it up? Could they recruit enough volunteers? How would they coordinate the effort?

AFTER DISCUSSIONS with Forward Sioux Falls committee members, Hanneman and Bohy developed a plan to set up a sort of mini telethon in Midco's large conference room over a one-week span. Hanneman asked Midco techs to install phone jacks around the conference room table and recruited eight volunteers to serve as callers who would follow a script to introduce the Forward Sioux Falls program, explain its goals, and encourage prospective investor leaders to pledge funds to support the effort. The callers would explain that Forward Sioux Falls was going to benefit everyone in the community, as each invested dollar would spread many times throughout the community. The message was, "We're moving Sioux Falls forward," and it's good for their business to move Sioux Falls forward.

Once a caller received a pledge, they'd hand the pledge card over to one of the 10 to 15 "runners" in a nearby room. The runner would jump up, run or drive to the business, and turn that pledge into an actual check. It was a fun way to drive immediate results, Hanneman said, and every pledge was important whether it was $25, $1,000, or $5,000.

"I don't think it was the large dollars," Hanneman said. "I think it was the message."

Forward Sioux Falls announced it had topped the $1 million mark by July, and by the time the fundraising campaign ended in September, the program shattered its goal by raising $1.8 million. The program's leaders created a vivid brochure to thank the hundreds of investors who each contributed between $25 and $75,000 to help usher in a new era of Sioux Falls.

"You were asked to think of tomorrow, to place in your mind a vision of what this community should be in the decades to come," the brochure said. "You did. And you backed that vision with your support."

Forward Sioux Falls' leaders knew they wanted to draw in new industry to continue the city economy's diversification, but they needed to narrow their targets to maximize investment. Previously, targets were selected based on hunches or past successful efforts. Forward Sioux Falls wanted to use a more researched-based scientific approach, so it hired The Boyd Company out of Princeton, New Jersey.

The firm spent several weeks in Sioux Falls to identify eight industries the community should target for future expansion and relocation. Jack Boyd, the firm's owner, noted in his report that competition for new industry in the Upper Midwest was "dog-eat-dog," but he identified key areas to pursue: medical products manufacturing, food processing, plastic products manufacturing, printing and publishing, health care and targeted office operations, electronics, fabricated metal products, and distribution warehousing.

Boyd noted Sioux Falls' number one opportunity was the medical industry, just as Sioux Valley Hospital began construc-

"YOU WERE ASKED TO THINK OF TOMORROW, TO PLACE IN YOUR MIND A VISION OF WHAT THIS COMMUNITY SHOULD BE IN THE DECADES TO COME."

tion of a new wellness center and Charter Medical broke ground on a new specialized psychiatric hospital. The report noted that a typical medical manufacturing plant could operate for $2.2 million less annually in Sioux Falls than in Minneapolis or $1.9 million less annually in Sioux Falls than in Chicago.

Meanwhile, the Chamber's Convention and Visitors Bureau commissioned California-based Alfred Gobar Associates to come up with a marketing plan to attract regional conventions of more than 200 attendees. The study included an examination of constraints that could be lifted through new facilities, broader access, or improved access.[1]

Forward Sioux Falls worked with the Lawrence & Schiller agency to launch its $640,000 coordinated national and regional marketing campaign, which took a balanced strategic approach to share Sioux Falls' story. The campaign included national and regional advertising and public relations, targeted marketing to the industries outlined in the Boyd report, and convention marketing to organizations outlined in the Gobar report.

The city was already showing results by the end of 1988, creating nearly 2,700 new jobs, hosting 62 new industrial prospects, generating 136 marketing responses, and issuing a record number of building permits. The financial services industry continued to flourish, with expansions at Sears Payment Systems and Service One International. Hutchinson Technology Inc., a Minnesota-based manufacturer of precision electronic components, announced it was opening a Sioux Falls factory to employ 250 people, and Wheeler Tank Manufacturing Inc.

[1] Gaumnitz, Lisa. "Official: Convention center needed." *Argus Leader*, April 13, 1991, accessed July 16, 2020 via Newspapers.com.

FORWARD SIOUX FALLS I — RESULTS ACHIEVED

6,200 JOBS created in the area

NEARLY $100 MILLION increase seen in the area's payroll

OVER $250 MILLION realized in new capital investment

5,000 TARGETED INDUSTRY REPORTS sent to corporate decision makers in five business categories

MADE PERSONAL CALLS to 115 new business prospects and hosted 235 prospects in Sioux Falls

relocated from St. Paul, Minnesota, to take over 22,000 square feet at Sioux Empire Industrial Park.

By the start of 1990, Sioux Falls had added 4,316 jobs and generated non-residential capital investment of $146.2 million, crushing the initial Forward Sioux Falls goal of $105 million during the program's full four-year run. The program continued to generate leads from business prospects, and the city's outlook for retail expansion was strong.

As the city's initial economic development initiative wrapped its successful run in 1991, Schroeder praised its impressive achievements.

"No matter how you measure its impact, Forward Sioux Falls has helped keep a good thing going for Sioux Falls," committee members proclaimed in a brochure sent to investors. "It's happened because there was a plan ... and a commitment to carry it out. Forward Sioux Falls has been an effective catalyst for new business development and renewed optimism about the city's future."

Forward Sioux Falls was riding the momentum wave, though additional challenges began to emerge as the city entered a new decade. Community leaders began exploring how current and future employers could find employees needed to fill all of the city's new positions, and they vowed to integrate higher education and training into future economic development efforts, said Roger Hainje, then Forward Sioux Falls president.

"Intellectual capital will be the driving force of economic development in the '90s," Hainje told the Argus Leader.[2]

[2] Schmidt, Brenda Wade. "Investor encourages Forward Sioux Falls to hold onto 'magic'." *Argus Leader*, August 12, 1990, accessed July 16, 2020 via Newspapers.com.

1987 - 1991

HUNDREDS OF BUSINESS LEADS produced through an aggressive direct mail and advertising program to reposition Sioux Falls in the eyes of business leaders across the country

FAVORABLE COVERAGE of the Sioux Falls business climate in major U.S. daily newspapers and in 19 trade publications

SIOUX FALLS BRIEFING CENTER, a modern center for presenting Sioux Falls' best face, opened in 1992

CHAPTER 5

The Question

BY THE TIME the initial Forward Sioux Falls program wrapped up its four-year run in 1991, it had created 6,200 new jobs and generated more than $250 million in capital for new construction projects.[1] Sioux Falls was regularly presenting itself in national newspapers and trade publications as a vibrant and growing community, and leaders diligently explored how to target new business sectors and attract larger conventions.

Forward Sioux Falls boasted impressive achievements, "even beyond those envisioned by its originators," said Lyle Schroeder, the initiative's campaign chairman.

But what was next? Forward Sioux Falls had a defined end date, yet the Sioux Falls business community wanted to continue moving the city forward. Community leaders galvanized into one cohesive force determined to attract new jobs and investment, and more work was ahead.

"As we were successful and people were discovering Sioux Falls, we could see this healthy business climate continuing forward," said Tony Bour, a cabinetry business owner who served on the Development Foundation board. "The local companies were starting to do better."

THE SIOUX FALLS BUSINESS COMMUNITY WANTED TO CONTINUE MOVING THE CITY FORWARD.

[1] Schmidt, Brenda Wade. "City program goes forward 4 more years: Forward Sioux Falls to enter a new phase." *Argus Leader*, June 6, 1991, accessed July 16, 2020 via Newspapers.com.

In 1991, a small group of business leaders gathered to ask the crucial question, "Are we going to do this again?" recalls the Chamber's Evan Nolte. Two of the city's top banking executives, First Bank of South Dakota President David Birkeland and Norwest Bank South Dakota President Gary Olson, said, "Of course. Why wouldn't we?"

"They knew that we needed to continue to replicate that success," Nolte said.

One prominent business leader sat silent before raising some doubt as to whether the program could raise that kind of money again, Nolte said. The group considered his point but recounted the many successes of the first program. The general climate of business was up, they argued, and people were feeling better about the city and its future.

THE PROGRAM WORKED BECAUSE IT FILLED A LEADERSHIP ROLE FOR THE SIOUX FALLS BUSINESS COMMUNITY.

Forward Sioux Falls had surpassed its goals, delivered results, and assured those who contributed that their pledges were truly investments in their community. The program worked because it filled a leadership role for the Sioux Falls business community, providing a unified approach to aggressively market the city, chart a course of action, and then move forward to get things done.

The decision was made to embark on Forward Sioux Falls II, and business leaders made their pitch in a brochure distributed to potential investors.

"Forward Sioux Falls II is needed to build on the success of the past four years," campaign leaders wrote. "Working together, it has been proven that a strong development plan gets results. Plus, today the leadership team is in place with a proven track record to keep Sioux Falls moving ahead."

During this time, the city benefitted from a growing coalition of business leaders that included locals who hailed from the region, second- and third-generation South Dakotans who returned to the state, and newcomers from such far-off places as New York and Arizona. Nolte said the community chose inclusion and collaboration over parochialism, as all were welcome at the table.

That inclusiveness continues today. Relationships are key, Nolte said, and he encourages future leaders not to wait for someone else to reach out to them before getting involved in the community. Bring your talent, network with others, and make a difference.

"When you're asked and you believe it fits, don't say 'No,'" Nolte said. "Say 'Yes.'"

FORWARD SIOUX FALLS continues to thrive as a sustainable venture because its leaders regularly say "Yes." The stakes are simply too high to fail, and Sioux Falls' business community has been successful in avoiding many of the common pitfalls that can lead to failure, said Howard Benson, the consultant from NCDS.

Benson, who has advised hundreds of cities across the nation, said such ventures can fail if they become simply "business as usual" or institutionalized to the point that they lose a sense of urgency. They can fail if they overreach by failing to perform due diligence when seeking input from business leaders. They can fail if the fundraising is looked upon as just another income stream. They can fail if they lose purpose and momentum by becoming a catch-all for every civic chore or an island of money in a sea of outstretched hands. And, specifically for Forward Sioux Falls, the program could fail if the Chamber and Development Foundation failed to cooperate and focused on protecting their turf.

Sioux Falls has consistently avoided these and other hazards that have hampered some other communities, Benson said.

"The good leaders will abandon ship about that time," he said. "What the good leaders want to do is move forward, accomplish things, hit the targets, and get the goals reached. They do not want to be around a passive organization."

Forward Sioux Falls eschews the "business as usual" trap by keeping its goals fresh and continually responding to community needs. The program vets current challenges and opportunities, shifts focus when it needs to, and attaches measurable and accountable goals to meet its objectives.

Bour said Forward Sioux Falls over the years has benefitted from charismatic leaders who consider where the city is today and where it's going to be 10 or 20 years down the road. They evaluate the city's needs and brainstorm ways that leaders can meet those needs. Bour encourages future leaders to be good listeners, communicate with purpose, and build consensus.

"Surround yourself with people who are smarter than you and listen to what they have to say," Bour said.

As Forward Sioux Falls' business leaders celebrated the successes of their first campaign, they encouraged the community to join together in a similar commitment to aggressively seek out and respond to new business opportunities: "All that's needed is your support... your commitment to another four years of progress."

The challenge was made—Forward Sioux Falls earned its sequel.

CHAPTER 6

Being #1 Matters

THE RESOUNDING SUCCESS of the first Forward Sioux Falls program confirmed to business leaders that they were on the right track placing Sioux Falls on the national radar.

Forward Sioux Falls II aimed to enhance its predecessor's marketing efforts while also tackling the issues of workforce expansion and education, government affairs, and retention and expansion of existing businesses. The program set a goal to create 6,000 new jobs producing $100 million in increased payroll and generate an additional $75 million annually in retail sales.

The centerpiece of the program was an expansion of marketing efforts that dedicated more than $1.1 million to promoting Sioux Falls. The specific initiatives included:

- A sharp, targeted approach marketing to industry groups
- Cost comparisons with other cities
- New advertising, updated direct mail, telemarketing, and aggressive public relations to attract favorable regional and national media attention
- A stronger emphasis on personal contact and hosting of prospects
- Updated research and presentation materials

- Incentives such as training assistance or building improvements
- Upgraded marketing materials to promote business conventions and visitors
- Continued promotion of Sioux Falls as a retail and medical center

Forward Sioux Falls II helped launch the South Dakota Port of Entry, providing a more convenient spot for foreign goods and passengers to clear US Customs.

The program also earmarked $300,000 for business retention and expansion efforts with a focus on uncovering factors that impede growth, providing local businesses with the same resources as out-of-town prospects, adding a staff professional to manage and coordinate business services, and developing a business resource center that offers seminars, counseling, and publications.

With Sioux Falls' unemployment rate by mid-1991 dropping to 2.6 percent—nearly four percentage points below the national average—it was becoming abundantly clear that Sioux Falls was going to have to transition some of its job creation efforts to *finding* people to fill those jobs.[1] Forward Sioux Falls II set aside $250,000 for workforce expansion and education to ensure a well-trained workforce for existing companies and new businesses. The program co-sponsored the Business Industry and Government (BIG) Job Fairs to attract skilled and semi-skilled employees and co-sponsored three high school job fairs attracting 40 businesses and 500 students.

The government affairs portion of the program allocated $100,000 to creating productive relationships between business and government. The research and communication efforts paid off with the 1994 defeat at the polls of Dakota 1, a property tax limitation that would have affected the economy and educational system. The funding also allowed the Chamber to provide the Sioux Falls area business community with continuous monitoring of local governmental issues and a strong and effective lobbying presence in Pierre.

[1] The Associated Press. "State jobless rate drops to 11-year low." *Argus Leader*, December 3, 1991, accessed July 16, 2020 via Newspapers.com.

The Joint Venture Management Committee set a fundraising goal of $2 million, and the business community again responded to the challenge with 354 investors contributing $2.2 million to exceed the bold goal.

Forward Sioux Falls II launched in 1992 and hit the jackpot by fall. In its September 1992 issue, *Money* magazine named Sioux Falls the best city to live in America, giving it a No. 1 rank among 300 of the nation's largest metropolitan areas.

Sioux Falls suddenly went from national obscurity to media darling. Phones at the Chamber and Development Foundation started ringing off the hook, overwhelming the two organizations' receptionists. Daily mail deliveries reaching two feet in height inundated the reception desks, and daily media requests poured in.

MONEY MAGAZINE NAMED SIOUX FALLS THE BEST CITY TO LIVE IN AMERICA.

"We weren't ready for it," Nolte said. "We had no conception what was going to happen when that ranking came out."

Nolte and Development Foundation President Roger Hainje decided that Forward Sioux Falls needed to speak as one voice, so they chose Hainje to serve as spokesman. The ranking thrust Hainje into the national spotlight through appearances on such popular programs as ABC's Good Morning America.

"Roger just embraced this," Nolte said. "This was the greatest opportunity for him."

To handle the onslaught of information requests mailed in from potential residents and out-of-town businesses, Nolte and Hainje reached out to Lawrence & Schiller co-founder Craig Lawrence. The trio and their staffs spent two and a half days developing an engaging handout to respond to the inquiries, and the Chamber and Development Foundation reception desks went from single-person operations to all-hands-on-deck response centers.

"Our goal was to try to have everything out of the office that same day," Nolte said.

The Chamber and Development Foundation even had to deal with occasional unannounced walk-ins.

"People were arriving in cars from out of town saying, 'I'm here!'" Nolte said. "It was like the oil boom in the early '80s in Denver."

Forward Sioux Falls II shifted some of its marketing campaign to capitalize on the Money ranking by mailing 5,000 reprints to business prospects. The program also took out two half-page ads in the Midwest and Los Angeles editions of USA Today, according to an Argus Leader story, to further spread the word.[2]

The accolade was the culmination of marketing efforts that launched with Forward Sioux Falls I, and it motivated the city's business leaders to reach out even further while continuing efforts to serve existing businesses. Although much focus was on diversifying the economy, business leaders in the spring of 1993 worried about the potential loss of one of Sioux Falls' largest employers, the John Morrell & Co. meatpacking plant.

With the plant's future in doubt, South Dakota Governor George Mickelson and several state and city leaders boarded the state plane and flew to Cincinnati to talk with company executives about saving the Sioux Falls plant and its 2,800 jobs. The contingent made its pitch and boarded the twin-engine turboprop for the return home, but the aircraft crashed in rain and fog near Dubuque, Iowa.

THE TRAGEDY CLAIMED THE LIVES of Governor Mickelson, South Dakota Office of Economic Development Commissioner Roland Dolly, state Office of Energy Policy Director Ron Reed, and three of Sioux Falls' most prominent business leaders: Hainje, First Bank of South Dakota President and CEO David Birkeland, and Northern States Power General Manager Angus Anson. State pilots Ron Becker and David Hansen also died in crash.

Hainje, 43, was the city's most visible economic development marketer, serving the Development Foundation since 1987. Mary Medema, Hainje's sister, described him as a tenacious leader and an excellent salesman when it came to selling the city he loved.

"His goal was to make sure we told the Sioux Falls story, no

"IT WAS LIKE THE OIL BOOM IN THE EARLY '80S IN DENVER."

[2] "City to advertise in 'USA Today'." *Argus Leader*, October 8, 1992, accessed July 16, 2020 via Newspapers.com.

matter what it took," said Medema, an HR executive who years later went on to lead the Sioux Falls Development Foundation's workforce development efforts.

The 54-year-old Birkeland, who served as chairman of the Sioux Falls Development Foundation, was a straightforward, no-nonsense leader who also donated time to the United Way, the YMCA, and Sioux Valley Hospital. Anson, 38, was an up-and-coming leader who was dedicated to improving his community.

Their deaths marked a terrible loss, Nolte said, as the men were more than just business colleagues; they were like family.

"That was the most devastating time that many of us can ever remember," he said. "That was a huge blow."

In the immediate days after the crash, Anson's employer, Northern States Power, generously made counselors available to Development Foundation staff and board members. The grieving continued through and after the funerals, as friends and colleagues regularly gathered and checked in on each other to see how they were feeling. And as the community healed, those working with Forward Sioux Falls vowed to honor those lost by continuing the economic development fight. Leaders such as Norwest Bank South Dakota President Gary Olson, a close friend of Birkeland who served as the Chamber's chairman, stepped up and led Forward Sioux Falls to redouble its efforts.

"There was a stronger dedication to not letting those people down," Nolte said.

Those working on Forward Sioux Falls II continued pushing the city forward to honor those lost. They embraced a longer-term view of economic development by initiating and serving as the primary funder of the Sioux Falls Tomorrow community-visioning process, mapping out what city stakeholders wanted to see achieved through 2015.

Forward Sioux Falls II also helped push the development and realization of the new Sioux Falls Convention Center and the Washington Pavilion of Arts and Science. City leaders chose to build the convention center west of the Sioux Falls arena and the creation of the performing arts center involved renovating a historic downtown building that formerly housed Washington High School.

In August 1993, city commissioners voted to issue sales tax revenue bonds of up to $33 million to fund construction of the two facilities, but the group Citizens for Responsible Spending referred the decision to a public vote, arguing that the projects would eventually raise property taxes. It seemed like 1985 all over again, but this time was different. In a dramatic about-face, "Red" Stangland, the TACCO group leader who a decade earlier had fought against building a $30 million convention center, performing arts center, and hotel in downtown Sioux Falls, lent his support to the effort.

Sioux Falls residents headed to the polls and approved the projects in October 1993 by 51.6 percent to 48.4 percent margin, and the city's pro-growth advocates continued building momentum. Dan Kirby, a founding member of the Washington Pavilion Board of Trustees, praised the city's forward-thinking attitude, saying, "The future called, and today Sioux Falls answered."

Crews broke ground on the Sioux Falls Convention Center in May 1995 and the 144,000 square-foot facility opened for business at the end of 1996 to host a range of events, conventions, and trade shows. (The building's first use was for a manufactured home show.) The convention center featured a 50,000 square-foot exhibit hall that could be divided into three large rooms and an additional 14 meeting rooms ranging in size from 400 to 1,300 square feet.

As construction projects continued throughout the city, more national accolades followed.

FORWARD SIOUX FALLS II — RESULTS ACHIEVED

MONEY MAGAZINE rated the Sioux Falls economy No. 1 in the nation in 1992, 1993, and 1994. Sioux Falls was named the "Best Place to Live in America" in 1992.

SIGNIFICANTLY INVOLVED in the realization of the Sioux Falls Convention Center and Washington Pavilion.

EXTENSIVE MARKETING efforts positioning Sioux Falls as a destination for conventions, special events, and other visitor business.

FORTIFIED THE CHAMBER'S PUBLIC AFFAIRS program to provide continuous monitoring of local governmental issues and a strong lobbying presence for the area's business community during the legislative session.

In 1995, *Biz* magazine ranked South Dakota at the head of the list of states best for business, and the following year, Redbook magazine named Sioux Falls one of the "10 Best Cities in the U.S. for Working Mothers."

Forward Sioux Falls was pushing the city forward, and the cumulative efforts of the first two programs shattered all goals by:

- Spurring a $662 million increase in capital investment (the combined goal was $105 million)
- Generating a $140 million increase in annual retail sales (the combined goal was $75 million)
- Prompting a 40- to 50-percent increase in awareness by regional and national corporate decision makers and opinion leaders (the combined goal was 20 percent)
- Creating 18,000 new jobs from business expansion and new business resulting in $349 million in increased wages and salaries (the combined goal was 12,000 jobs generating $190 million)

The faster-than-expected job creation rate marked an incredible success story, but it created additional challenges. Sioux Falls' unemployment rate dipped below 2 percent during 1996, and the area simply didn't have enough qualified employees to fill its growing opportunities. It was clear that future Forward Sioux Falls programs would have to devote even more significant resources to workforce development initiatives.

Forward Sioux Falls firmly established its value as it closed its first decade. The program overcame the tragic loss of several prominent business leaders, but others stepped up when they were needed most.

BIZ MAGAZINE RANKED SOUTH DAKOTA AT THE HEAD OF THE LIST OF STATES BEST FOR BUSINESS.

1992 - 1996

BUSINESS INDUSTRY AND GOVERNMENT (BIG) JOB FAIRS, as well as other job fairs, were co-sponsored by FSF II to attract skilled and semi-skilled employees. Business-Education Partnership Programs were expanded and FSF facilitated three high school job fairs attracting 40 businesses and 500 students.

SIOUX FALLS TOMORROW, a community-based planning process, was initiated and funded to develop a vision and goals for the city beginning in 2015.

RESEARCHED AND INFORMED THE PUBLIC about Dakota 1, a property tax limitation measure that would have harmed the economy and educational system; it was voted down.

CHAPTER 7

Into the Next Century

THE FIRST TWO FORWARD SIOUX FALLS PROGRAMS enjoyed overwhelming success, so as community business leaders began gathering in 1996 to discuss the possibility of a third economic development effort, the prospects seemed strong. Yet, they were not a given.

Some at the table considering the possibility of a Forward Sioux Falls III raised questions of "Should we do another?" and "Is the work done?" recalled Fred Slunecka, then president of Avera McKennan Hospital. A few leaders argued that many of the issues addressed by Forward Sioux Falls had long been resolved, and they questioned whether the program had served its role.

"No," the group concluded, and Slunecka agreed.

Some work might have been completed, but plenty of other tasks remained. The amazing addition of 18,000 jobs over the first two programs highlighted a need to strengthen workforce development efforts through training and education while continuing to support existing businesses and recruit new businesses. Forward Sioux Falls needed to increase the community's investment in technology, enhance and preserve residents' quality of life, and promote the community's business-friendly status.

Economic development isn't a short-term endeavor, and prospering communities don't rest on their laurels. The Joint Venture Management Committee held a news conference on October 31, 1996, to unveil "*Forward Sioux Falls—Into the Next Century.*"[1]

"Now you could see that this wasn't going to be a one-time or two-time event," Slunecka said. "This was now going to be an ongoing, living, breathing exercise that the community would engage in every five years where there would be a formal planning process, a commitment, and a follow-through."

Forward Sioux Falls—Into the Next Century set an aggressive goal to create 10,000 new jobs while devoting significant resources to workforce development so the city could fill those jobs. Specifically, the city's business leaders set out to:

- Promote workforce development resulting in the education and training of a minimum of 1,000 workers
- Enhance the retention and expansion of existing business and industry
- Attract and recruit new business and industry from selected target markets including the medical field, agricultural processing, information systems, and financial services
- Assess the city's technology resources and needs
- Lead and advocate the preservation of a business-friendly climate in Sioux Falls and the state of South Dakota
- Enhance and preserve the quality of life through the development of more affordable housing and support for economic development and community improvement projects that will establish and maintain Sioux Falls as a regional center

Leaders set an even higher fundraising bar by putting a $3 million price tag on the program. They sought $50,000 to $250,000 from top prospects before proceeding to a second stage for $10,000 to $50,000 investors and a third stage for $2,000 to $10,000 investors.

Bluestem Capital Company Founding Partner Steve Kirby, who had completed his term as South Dakota's lieutenant gover-

> "THIS WAS NOW GOING TO BE AN ONGOING, LIVING, BREATHING EXERCISE THAT THE COMMUNITY WOULD ENGAGE IN EVERY FIVE YEARS."

[1] Swenson, Rob. "Forward Sioux Falls objective: 10,000 jobs." *Argus Leader*, November 1, 2006, accessed July 16, 2020 via Newspapers.com.

nor a year earlier, served on the Forward Sioux Falls III advance team. He said many potential investors were so confident in the program that they nearly had their checks written out before committee members reached the lobby. For others, the team shared information about the success of the first two programs.

Dana Dykhouse, who would go on to co-chair Forward Sioux Falls V and VI, was a 28-year-old loan officer when he was tapped to expand the base of investors by recruiting small businesses and individual donors to the Forward Sioux Falls III campaign. Dykhouse recalls the strong leadership shown by Campaign Chair Gary Olson, president of Norwest Bank South Dakota, who kicked off the fundraising effort by announcing significant investments by both his employer and him personally.

"When he was willing to take the leadership role, train us how to do it, be the lead gift and give personally, boy that set the tone for all of us," said Dykhouse, the president and CEO of First PREMIER Bank. "And every campaign I've been on since, I have made certain that if I'm going to lead the campaign, we're going to have the lead gift."

Forward Sioux Falls—Into the Next Century blew the top off its goal by raising more than $4.2 million from 446 investors. Everybody dug deep to make meaningful gifts toward the effort, Kirby said.

"It's just another example of the Sioux Falls community embracing an effort that is totally contrary to what goes on in the United States of America," Kirby said. "The vast majority of giving was from small businesses and individuals."

BUSINESS LEADERS QUICKLY REALIZED that they faced new challenges due in part to Forward Sioux Falls' past successes. The city had more jobs than willing applicants, and it needed to devote significant resources to developing the city's workforce. Forward Sioux Falls set reasonable milestones to do everything humanly possible to identify anyone who was a prospective worker.

The Sioux Falls Development Foundation created the Workforce Development Council under Dan Scott's leadership. Mary Medema was hired in 1998 as Workforce Development Director, a position funded by Forward Sioux Falls.

Medema, who spent 18 years as a human resource executive in the grocery store industry, was a longtime Chamber volunteer who knew many of the city's business leaders and nearly all of the city's HR managers. She viewed her job as a connector, and for two decades she connected employers across the business community with potential employees and educational institutions rich with students who could fill jobs.

When Medema was new in her position, a technical recruiter from Sencore approached her noting the difficulty in filling some of the company's high-tech job vacancies. Medema realized that many companies faced similar struggles, so she helped launch the Sioux Falls Recruiting Cooperative to connect 23 employers with extremely specific skill needs so they could develop shared resources.

The eclectic group featured recruiters from health care, manufacturing, engineering, call centers, and technical firms who wondered how they could more consistently feature their companies and their high-end technical positions. The co-op mailed more than 2,000 postcards to former South Dakotans to make them aware of the high-tech and professional career opportunities in Sioux Falls. It launched a website allowing employers to list position openings and jobseekers to upload their résumés.

Much of Medema's early workforce development efforts centered on education, as Forward Sioux Falls sought to ensure the city had an educational system nimble enough to react to the needs of the community. She helped create and promote ShadowED, which over its 19-year run offered more than 4,600 high school students the chance to work a half-day alongside professionals from local businesses in hundreds of occupations. Forward Sioux Falls also highlighted school-to-work initiatives and supported the creation of the University Center on the Southeast Technical Institute campus. Forward Sioux Falls also helped expand blue-collar job opportunities by supporting Southeast Tech's community welding training program and the Academy for the Construction Trades, a summer training and employment program for senior high school students and graduates to develop skills related to the construction industry.

Though connections in workforce development are key, Forward Sioux Falls' continued marketing efforts over the years also played a big part in growing the community's workforce. The more the program promoted Sioux Falls as a great place to live, work, and play, the easier it became to encourage employees and their families to relocate.

FORWARD SIOUX FALLS— INTO THE NEXT CENTURY EXCEEDED ITS GOALS.

"The features that make us attractive to visitors are also those features that make us attractive to any newcomer—those things you can do as a family, those things that entertain us, those things that make us feel safe," Medema said.

The Forward Sioux Falls Technology committee, chaired by Sioux Valley Hospitals and Health System Executive Vice President Dave Link, set a bold goal: "To establish Sioux Falls as the geographic and economic center of a regional high technology corridor by fully utilizing and marketing our existing technology resources and identifying and exceeding the needs of current and future technology-based businesses."

The more than 30 committee members launched a Technology Resources Inventory and Needs Assessment (TRINA) study, conducted a technology education availability inventory, and explored ways to augment existing Forward Sioux Falls technology workforce development efforts.

Forward Sioux Falls—Into the Next Century exceeded its goals by creating 14,531 new jobs, generating more than $724 million in commercial construction, and recording a 23 percent increase in business located in Sioux Empire Development Parks. The program also:

- Worked with Avera McKennan Hospital, the Sioux Empire Housing Partnership, the Sioux Falls Development Foundation, and a coalition of suppliers and homebuilders to help create the Lacey Park neighborhood with 40 residential lots
- Helped develop the Employer Mortgage Assistance Program (EMAP), an effort co-sponsored by the Sioux Empire Housing Partnership and the South Dakota Housing Development Authority. The program offered down payment assistance to help create affordable housing opportunities
- Launched the www.siouxfalls.com portal to serve as the online home for the Chamber, the Development Foundation, and the Sioux Falls Convention & Visitors Bureau
- Supported construction of the Falls Park Visitor Information Center and Observation Tower, which opened on Memorial Day weekend 1999. The center welcomed more than 50,000 signed-in guests from 48 states and 26 foreign counties during its inaugural summer.
- Provided local matching funds to assist with the state's purchase of more than 200 acres within the Blood Run historical site, land along the valley of the Big Sioux River that would eventually become part of South Dakota's first new state park in more than 40 years

Gary Olson declared the third Forward Sioux Falls program a success, putting Sioux Falls and the surrounding area on a course where job creation and community growth are the result.

"The Sioux Falls area is dominant economically in the region," Olson said. "Our diversified economy is admired and

FORWARD SIOUX FALLS III — RESULTS ACHIEVED

THE WORKFORCE DEVELOPMENT COUNCIL was created to promote workforce and job opportunities, as well as general information about Sioux Falls.

LACEY PARK NEIGHBORHOOD In an effort to increase the supply of housing for low-to-moderate income buyers, Avera McKennan Hospital, The Sioux Empire Housing Partnership, Sioux Falls Development Foundation and other stakeholders created the Lacey Park neighborhood. Phase 1 of the project involved moving 20 homes.

studied by communities from the Twin Cities to Denver. The hard work done to get us to this point is cause for celebration and reflection, but we must not lessen our efforts to grow, innovate, and improve."

Meanwhile, the city continued to compile accolades:

- Ladies' Home Journal in March 2000 ranked Sioux Falls seventh in the nation for best bets for working women, and the April 2000 issue of Modern Maturity ranked the city as one of the 10 best places to live.
- The May 2000 issue of Forbes ranked Sioux Falls among the top 25 of the nation's best places to do business and advance a career based on comparisons of wage and salary growth, job growth, and the growth of high technology.
- A Cognetics Inc. analysis published in the April 2001 edition of Kiplinger Report ranked Sioux Falls third in a national list of top cities to start a company.
- Sioux Falls received an A+ on Zero Population Growth's 2001 Kid-Friendly Cities Report Card by excelling in health, public safety, education, economics, environment, and community life.
- Sales and Marketing Management placed Sioux Falls at No. 4 on the list of 20 Hottest Cities for Selling in 1999.
- Builder magazine identified Sioux Falls as one of the Next Big Growth Markets for residential building.

With Forward Sioux Falls now an established, ongoing effort, the city was continuing to prosper. Now it was time to take that success to the next level.

1997 - 2001

THE EMPLOYER MORTGAGE ASSISTANCE PROGRAM (EMAP) was developed to create affordable housing opportunities in the Sioux Falls area to ensure a growing workforce. Co-sponsored by the SEHP and the South Dakota Housing Development Authority, EMAP helps businesses give their employees who are first-time homebuyers funds to aid in the purchase of their home.

2000 U.S. CENSUS FIGURES showed that from 1990 to 2000 Minnehaha County experienced a 19.8 percent growth rate, while Lincoln County experienced a 56.4 percent growth rate.

LINCOLN COUNTY was the fastest growing county in the country for percentage change in housing units from 2000-2003, according to the U.S. Census Bureau.

CHAPTER 8

Taking Success to the Next Level

THE COMMITTEE TAKING THE BATON for the fourth leg of Forward Sioux Falls set an aggressive fundraising goal of $5.5 million, so it tasked a trio of heavy hitters to recruit fellow business colleagues to pledge support.

Forward Sioux Falls IV—Taking Success to the Next Level named Avera McKennan Hospital Regional President Fred Slunecka, Sioux Valley Hospitals and Health System President and CEO Kelby Krabbenhoft, and Wells Fargo Senior Vice President Cathy Clark as co-chairs of the campaign development council.

Clark said showing up at a potential investor's office with the top executives from the region's most influential healthcare organizations sent a compelling message that the stakes were high.

"How powerful is it for the two of them to walk into a company and say, 'We need your time; we need your investment'?" she asked.

The three leaders were asking for significant investments, so it was important for them to bring facts and figures to back up their solicitations. Investors want to study the history of past programs, they want to see how those programs provided return on investment, and they want to hear assurances of accountability, Slunecka said.

"When we're asking our fellow community leaders to make very large donations, it's done with the attitude that we're going to be good stewards of that money," he said. "We're going to do exactly what we promised—nothing more, nothing less."

But beyond the facts and figures, business leaders who approach investors must share the Forward Sioux Falls story to connect with investors on a more personal level, Clark said.

"IT GOES BEYOND THE BUSINESS."

"It goes beyond the business," she said. "It goes to their employees. It goes to their spouse. It goes to their children. How are we making this community better for all of them?"

Clark, Slunecka, and Krabbenhoft knocked it out of the park, raising $6.4 million from 412 investors to shatter the bold goal, prompting praise from Forward Sioux Falls IV general campaign chair Tom Everist.

"This measure of success indicates one thing," said Everist, President and CEO of L.G. Everist, Inc. "This community realizes the importance of continuing to move forward—and is willing to invest in that effort, showing confidence and belief in our future together."

Clark, Slunecka, and Krabbenhoft were some of the community's most powerful business leaders, and it would have been easy for any of them to say that they're too busy for such commitments. Yet each stepped up and freely gave of their time, spending countless hours going from business to business to bring additional investors on board, said Bluestem Capital Company Founding Partner Steve Kirby.

"All three of those leaders didn't just do what was asked of them. They went way above and beyond," Kirby said. "There were weeks that that was their full-time job. That's all they did, was get in their car and go to the next stop and the next stop."

Clark said the teamwork displayed between Slunecka and

Krabbenhoft demonstrated how business leaders who competed by day could come together when the good of Sioux Falls was on the line. All three of the campaign development council chairs were demonstrative and engaged in lively debate, but those discussions were always done with respect. They didn't necessarily agree on everything, but they always found common ground, Clark said.

"It was all about, 'How do we lift the community?'" she said. "Because in the long run, we all win from that, and they win from that as well."

Similar collaboration could be seen in the banking industry. Dana Dykhouse, the president and CEO of First PREMIER Bank, spent four decades competing with Bill Baker of The First National Bank in Sioux Falls for business clients. But if a project ever surfaced that could better the community, Dykhouse could call his friend and know Baker would never say no. And the same worked in reverse.

"We compete daily for businesses," Dykhouse said. "We're very competitive, citywide, statewide, and nationally, but when it comes to what's best for Sioux Falls, everybody will instantly pull together. I would hate that we would ever lose that. That is something that has just been a hallmark of Sioux Falls going forward."

Everist, writing in his initial campaign prospectus, praised the past three Forward Sioux Falls efforts for achieving success through partnership, planning, and persistence, and he challenged potential investors to bring that commitment into a new and changing world.

"Business moves faster. Technologies are constantly changing," Everist said. "Young people face so many choices—and our community must work harder to take our success to the next level."

Forward Sioux Falls IV stood ready to address the areas of workforce development, business attraction and retention, community and business climate improvements, and technology enhancements by:

- Promoting the Sioux Falls area as a region of "opportunity" for job seekers, actively participating in the education and training of the workforce, and enhancing business resources to address workforce challenges and opportunities
- Assisting the efforts of established and new business to create positive growth through focused regional partnerships in workforce development, economic advancement, and maintenance of critical land assets
- Enhancing Sioux Falls' excellent quality of life through emphasis on affordable housing initiatives and the fostering of regional partnerships
- Fostering regional economic growth and diversification through the expansion and development of technology-based businesses in the Sioux Falls area

Within a year of the Forward Sioux Falls IV launch, the city suddenly found itself serving a larger market.

In 2003, the federal Office of Management and Budget added McCook and Turner counties to the Sioux Falls Metropolitan Statistical Area (MSA), hoisting it over the 200,000-resident milestone. The feds had always included Minnehaha and Lincoln counties in the Sioux Falls MSA, and they made the change after realizing that 25 percent of McCook and Turner residents commuted to Sioux Falls for work.[1]

The adjustment highlighted the need for the area to continue developing its workforce.

[1] Kirschenmann, Jay. "Hey Turner and McCook, how does it feel to be 'metro?'." *Argus Leader*, July 21, 2003, accessed July 16, 2020 via Newspapers.com.

FORWARD SIOUX FALLS IV made significant investments in technology and entrepreneurship, drawing on the findings of the Technology Resources Inventory and Needs Assessment

(TRINA) commissioned during Forward Sioux Falls—Into the Next Century (1997-2001). The recommendations sought to improve the area's ability to grow, attract, and retain high-tech firms and innovative entrepreneurs.

Rich Naser, a Forward Sioux Falls Technology Committee member, said the goal was to further diversify Sioux Falls' economy and bring in higher-paying jobs. The study looked at the human capital resources in the region and identified between 45,000 and 50,000 students who could fill jobs in the technology space.

"It doesn't matter if you have the equity. It doesn't matter if you have the innovation," Naser said. "If you can't get the people that you need to help translate that into a company, you're not going to grow here."

The study identified 15 technology needs in the areas of labor availability, marketing and promotion, telecommunications infrastructure, and the need for new facilities to serve the technology and entrepreneurial communities. Specifically, the study called for establishment of a business incubator/accelerator, a university-affiliated research center to foster relationships between private companies and educational institutions, and a sprawling research park to foster entrepreneurship and commercialization for innovation-based businesses.

It was clear that the research center and research park were longer-term goals, as they'd require partnering with such entities as the State of South Dakota, federal government grant agencies, and the state Board of Regents. Yet technology committee members felt Forward Sioux Falls could take the lead in establishing a business incubator/accelerator, so they proposed launching the South Dakota Technology Business Center (SDTBC) in northwest Sioux Falls near the Southeast Tech campus.

When crews broke ground on the SDTBC in 2003, the 38,000 square-foot facility was hailed as the first step in an ongoing effort to support the creation and expansion of technology-based businesses and the entrepreneurs who launch them. Forward Sioux Falls put the center under the joint direction of the Sioux Falls Chamber and Sioux Falls Development Foundation and hired Naser as the SDTBC's first executive director.

"We decided that it was appropriate for the business community to focus on entrepreneurship, business development, and innovation," Naser said. "We thought we could get our arms around that and actually make that happen."

As the SDTBC opened its doors in January 2004, Everist declared the moment as the beginning of a new era for Sioux Falls business growth. The center, since renamed the Zeal Center for Entrepreneurship, offered office, lab, and light manufacturing space with flexible leases of up to three years. Its first two clients were Prairie Gold Venture Partners, a private equity firm, and DocuTAP, an electronic medical records firm.

"We filled it up within two to three years," Naser said.

DocuTAP in its early days was a one-person firm, with founder Eric McDonald working 12-hour days to grow his client base and expand his business, Naser said. The center helped McDonald connect with investors and provided such needed infrastructure as phone lines, internet connectivity, and a Microsoft Exchange server. An intern at SDTBC created the company's first logo.

"Eric was a true entrepreneur," said Mary Medema, the Sioux Falls Development Foundation's workforce development director. "He was just doing everything himself, and he was the only employee."

As DocuTAP added employees and broadened its market by targeting the growing urgent care trend, the company outgrew its space and moved out of the South Dakota Technology Business Center in 2007. The company received national recognition when the National Business Incubator Association

IT WAS HAILED AS THE FIRST STEP IN AN ONGOING EFFORT TO SUPPORT THE CREATION AND EXPANSION OF TECHNOLOGY-BASED BUSINESSES AND THE ENTREPRENEURS WHO LAUNCH THEM.

named DocuTAP its 2009 Graduate of the Year in the technology category.[2]

DocuTAP had to move back into the SDTBC after facing some ups and downs due to the death of a prime investor and the 2008 recession. It eventually overcame the challenges, jumped on the touch-tablet device trend, and re-graduated out of the center in 2014, moving into downtown office space on Phillips Avenue. The company grew to nearly 300 employees before merging with Illinois-based Practice Velocity in 2019 to form Experity.

FORWARD SIOUX FALLS IV also continued workforce development initiatives in an effort to increase the city's labor force by 8,000. The program promoted job opportunities online to 60,000 students within a five-state region and a million adults from across the country. It launched the Interns in Industry program in 2003 to promote full-time paid summer internships to students studying on campuses throughout the region. Companies paid for the internships, but Forward Sioux Falls kicked in scholarships for the students.

Forward Sioux Falls partnered with the Sioux Falls Recruiting Cooperative to attract out-of-state technical professionals and experts from other fields. The need for technology expertise was continuing to expand, and technology was also changing how businesses interacted with both clients and potential employees. Medema used to say that the best place to learn about a business was in their lobby, because that's where candidates first discovered how a company would treat you.

"Then the lobby became their website," she said. "That's how both applicants and customers have interacted with those companies ever since."

To cultivate the region's home-grown tech talent, the Forward Sioux Falls Technology Committee joined forces with area edu-

[2] "Alumni," Startup Sioux Falls, accessed July 16, 2020, https:// www.startupsiouxfalls.com/ zeal/alumni/

cation providers to expand technology education and training. The committee also expanded the number and variety of internship opportunities, creating links between area businesses and students studying in Sioux Falls area colleges and technical institutes. Other programs supported career development and awareness efforts in K-12 facilities.

Forward Sioux Falls IV continued taking success to the next level by creating 6,872 new jobs, beginning the city's journey into entrepreneurship and technology, and continuing to improve the city's business friendly reputation.

FORWARD SIOUX FALLS IV — RESULTS ACHIEVED

SOUTH DAKOTA TECHNOLOGY BUSINESS CENTER Opened for business in January 2004, the SDTBC's mission is to diversify and expand the regional economy by providing "best practices" incubator services and networking opportunities to qualified new and early-stage technology-based companies.

6,902 BUILDING PERMITS were issued by the City of Sioux Falls in 2004, with a value of $409 million.

THE INTERNS IN INDUSTRY PROGRAM was formed to create links between area businesses and students currently studying in Sioux Falls area colleges and technical institutes and ultimately grow the area's skilled workforce.

LARGE COMMUNITY OF THE YEAR South Dakota Gov. Mike Rounds recognized Sioux Falls as the Large Community of the Year in 2006.

2002 - 2006

1.7% UNEMPLOYMENT By the end of the first quarter of 2001, the unemployment rate in Sioux Falls was 1.7 percent, compared to 2.2 percent statewide and 4.3 percent nationwide.

FASTEST GROWING COUNTY IN THE COUNTRY According to the U.S. Census Bureau, Lincoln County was the fastest growing county in the country for percentage change in housing units from 2000-2003.

FASTEST-CHANGING METRO AREA IN THE NATION A 2001 study by the Center for Immigration Studies, a Washington, D.C.-based nonprofit research group, found that Minnehaha County was the fastest-changing metro area in the nation, based on the population's 125 percent increase of foreign-born people from 1990-1998.

CHAPTER 9

Bold New Perspectives

THE TECHNOLOGY AND ENTREPRENEURSHIP initiatives advanced in the third and fourth editions of Forward Sioux Falls took front-and-center seats for "Forward Sioux Falls V — Bold New Perspectives," with the launch of a workforce marketing campaign targeting 17- to 30-year-olds and expansion of the South Dakota Technology Business Center (now the Zeal Center for Entrepreneurship).

When campaign co-chair Dana Dykhouse first got involved with Forward Sioux Falls back in the late 1990s, the city was the land of "cheap labor, cheap land, and cheap insurance costs," he said. But as other communities started giving away land and other incentives to draw new residents and workers, Sioux Falls leaders began to realize that they were going to have to focus on the city's best asset—its intellectual capital.

Forward Sioux Falls V shifted workforce development marketing to attracting 17- to 30-year-olds, pivoting into a more digital-based marketing campaign. Stay Close-Go Far targeted tens of thousands of young adults within a 200-mile radius of Sioux Falls with an original song, a dedicated website, and a message touting Sioux Falls' advantages and opportunities to work, play,

SIOUX FALLS LEADERS BEGAN TO REALIZE THAT THEY WERE GOING TO HAVE TO FOCUS ON THE CITY'S BEST ASSET—ITS INTELLECTUAL CAPITAL.

and learn. The campaign branded Sioux Falls as an "Opportunity City" where young people could live, work, and continue their education, and the campaign prompted nearly 3,000 e-newsletter signups before making its move to Facebook in 2010.

"Young people used to decide where's the job and I'll move there," Dykhouse said. "Now they say, 'Where do I want to live and what opportunities do I have there?'"

That was a big shift from the late '90s. Employers during this era were growing adept at targeting workers, selling their companies' benefits, and widening their perspective of the talent pool. Job seekers were expecting more, and the most successful employers met those expectations.

Forward Sioux Falls V set a fundraising goal of $8.5 million, and campaign co-chairs Dykhouse and Kelby Krabbenhoft exceeded that goal by $2 million, raising a total of $10.5 million—an astronomical jump from the $6.4 million raised in Forward Sioux Falls IV.

Forward Sioux Falls V devoted more than $2 million to the South Dakota Technology Business Center (SDTBC), which upgraded its telecommunications and data network infrastructure in 2009 and added 7,000 square feet of new space to include conference rooms, in-bound and out-bound call center functionality, and some lab space. It added a client service manager, enhanced its focus on business development assistance to early-stage ventures, expanded its education programs, added new networking opportunities, and established a week-long tech boot camp. A $1.24 million federal Economic Development Administration grant funded the majority of the expansion, and both the Chamber and Development Foundation kicked in for the local match.

The SDTBC continued graduating an impressive list of companies that included Meta Payment Systems, a division of MetaBank focusing on prepaid cards, credit products, electronic funds transfer, and ATMs. Meta Payment Systems needed a data room to process its transactions, so it asked SDTBC Executive Director Rich Naser if he could add one to the center.

Crews got to work installing HVAC and fire suppression equipment and converted a small room into a climate-controlled data center, charging Meta a small monthly fee for the infrastructure. Within 18 months, the company outgrew the SDTBC space and became its latest graduate. During the entire Forward Sioux Falls V program, the center created 339 jobs with an average salary of $70,000 and saw 11 patents awarded to its companies.

Dykhouse said Sioux Falls has a track record of hundreds of small entrepreneurial businesses that have grown, succeeded, and contributed. They might not draw the publicity a community would get when announcing a new auto plant or a giant distribution center that employs thousands, but each has helped Sioux Falls grow job by job.

"And I think that's the secret," Dykhouse said. "It diversifies our economy. It makes certain when a downturn comes, it doesn't hit the entire community."

Forward Sioux Falls V supported the 2009 opening of the 21,000 square-foot Graduate Education and Applied Research (GEAR) Center at University Center, designed to stimulate applied research and commercialization in South Dakota. The center, built on a section of land in northwest Sioux Falls destined to become part of a larger university research park, paired the University of South Dakota Biomedical Engineering Program with two companies, AlphaGenix and Antimicrobial Technologies Group (ATG). The GEAR Center now boasts some $4 million in high-tech equipment to help science and engineering startups grow and commercialize their innovations.

When the Great Recession hit the US in 2008, Sioux Falls was in a better position to weather the storm than communities of similar and larger sizes, and that strength continues today. In a 2020 study, SmartAsset ranked Sioux Falls as No. 10 in the nation in its ranking of recession-resistant cities.[1]

[1] Ahmad, Nadia, "Most Recession-Resistant Cities – 2020 Edition," SmartAsset, March 5, 2020, accessed July 16, 2020, https://smartasset.com/checking-account/most-recession-resistant-cities-2020

Workforce development efforts continued during this period, with Forward Sioux Falls partnering with 38 businesses to offer 135 internships and award $67,500 in scholarships. ShadowED continued connecting high school students with industry, offering more than 1,600 kids the chance to work a half-day alongside professionals from 120 local business in more than 250 occupations.

Dykhouse said Forward Sioux Falls' workforce initiatives likely have had the greatest impact on Sioux Falls over the years.

"It all comes down to the number of jobs within that community," Dykhouse said. "You don't build new houses, you don't occupy new apartment buildings, you don't fill new restaurants without people having jobs that they can take that payroll and utilize that for consumer spending."

EDUCATIONAL OPPORTUNITIES in Sioux Falls and nine surrounding districts took a big leap forward in the fall of 2010 with the opening of the Career & Technical Education Academy. The new Sioux Falls School District facility built near the Southeast Tech campus offered high school students never-before-available courses in such specialized fields as biomedical and health science; architecture and construction; science, technology, engineering, and math (STEM); hospitality and tourism; arts; audio/visual technology and communication; transportation, distribution, and logistics; electronics/manufacturing; and human services. Forward Sioux Falls' workforce development program was tapped to help connect the worlds of education and business to support the new endeavor.

Forward Sioux Falls V also helped the Chamber create the Sioux Falls Young Professionals Network (YPN), which aims to cultivate an informed and involved young professional community in the Sioux Falls area to retain and attract young and diverse talent. YPN creates opportunities for young professionals aged 21-39 to network with peers via mixers, interact with community leaders through its Seat at the Table programs, and engage in civic and professional development.

Lucas Fiegen joined YPN in 2012 after returning to Sioux Falls upon graduation from the University of Nebraska-Lincoln. Fiegen said young professionals often have to bide their time and wait until they're in a leadership position to have a say in community involvement and growth.

YPN helps young professionals find their voices, "giving them a network to collaborate amongst one another, but also getting themselves ingrained within the bigger community picture, the bigger Chamber picture," said Fiegen, vice president of Fiegen Construction Co.

YPN's efforts eventually led to Sioux Falls being recognized for three consecutive years as the No. 1 city in the nation for young professionals.

SIOUX FALLS WAS RECOGNIZED FOR THREE CONSECUTIVE YEARS AS THE NO. 1 CITY IN THE NATION FOR YOUNG PROFESSIONALS.

On the advocacy front, Forward Sioux Falls leveraged resources to maintain an economically viable tax structure while encouraging cooperation among business and government leaders on program development and implementation. Chamber lobbyists supported South Dakota's congressional delegation funding of the Lewis & Clark Regional Water System, a continued presence of Air and Army National Guard facilities and missions, and enhanced air service through the Sioux Falls Regional Airport Authority.

In 2007, a Military Task Force was created by resolution, which once again demonstrated the Forward Sioux Falls culture and collaborative spirit between the Chamber and Development Foundation. The Task Force's purpose, to secure and advance the missions of our military units both in Sioux Falls and South Dakota, brought together leaders from both the public and private sector to champion such initiatives as the preservation of Ellsworth Air Force Base, advocacy for basing the F-35 Joint Strike Fighter, as well as establishing fly-ins to Washington, D.C. to meet with South

Dakota's congressional delegation. Under the leadership of Retired Brigadier General Ron Mielke and Retired Brigadier General R.J. Clifft, the Military Task Force remains steadfast in its efforts to advocate and preserve military units in our area.

Forward Sioux Falls has consistently supported the Airport Authority over the years, and it stepped up its efforts in 2011 by forming an Air Service Committee. Under the leadership of Avera McKennan Hospital Regional President and CEO Dr. Dave Kapaska, the committee worked with Airport Authority Executive Director Dan Letellier to recruit new airlines, promote competition, and encourage existing providers to add routes.

The committee and the Airport Authority also teamed up to combat a growing public relations issue known as airport leakage. For years, residents in and around Sioux Falls often drove to Omaha or Minneapolis to save $50 or $100 on an airline ticket, completely ignoring the value of their time, the fuel cost of driving hundreds of miles, or the rate of an overnight motel room stay, Dykhouse said. Forward Sioux Falls helped the authority educate residents of the true savings and benefits in flying out of Sioux Falls, dropping Sioux Falls Regional Airport's leakage rate from 45 percent in 2008 to 17 percent in 2018.

"Not only did we bring more competition and lower prices to Sioux Falls, but we actually, by bringing that up as an issue, changed the attitude of some of the business travelers and other travelers," Dykhouse said.

Business leaders also lobbied to support the Quality of Life II Bond Issue of July 2009, which funded improvements for the Great Plains Zoo & Delbridge Museum, a new west-side library, an expansion of the Big Sioux River Greenway, and a youth sports complex for South Dakota Junior Football. Forward Sioux Falls V also helped lobby the Sioux Falls City Council to level off the second-penny sales tax, which took effect at the start of 2009 to help fund the city's arterial street system and water distribution lines.

The Sioux Empire Housing Partnership (SEHP) expanded

its reach to the entire Sioux Falls metro area. Forward Sioux Falls helped the partnership purchase land for Valley Green Development to build 49 homes with an average selling price of $115,000 and build five new condominium units as part of the Pettigrew Heights Revitalization Program.

Forward Sioux Falls V continued the program's successes by adding 7,050 jobs while spurring nearly $2 billion in construction and more than $1 billion in capital investment.

Consulting firm National Community Development Services (NCDS), in preparing a 2010 report for the next Forward Sioux Falls initiative, praised the city for building a strong, diverse economy.

"Unemployment is low, the cost of living is moderate, and recreational opportunities are abundant," NCDS CEO Howard Benson wrote in the report.

But Benson warned of several challenges that needed to be confronted. The area competed with low-wage overseas manufacturing jobs, faced competition for its talented young workers, and had to navigate the impacts of national financial regulations. He urged business leaders to focus on creating new, well-paying jobs, enlist new leadership to help implement the next program, and take a more regional approach toward economic development.

TO SET A COURSE for the next 20 years and beyond, Forward Sioux Falls teamed with the City of Sioux Falls, Minnehaha and Lincoln Counties, the Sioux Falls Area Community Foundation, and the Sioux Empire United Way to embark on Future Sioux Falls, an economic development planning process to enhance economic development activities and programs. The team hired Atlanta-based Market Street Services to develop a comprehensive study to continue expanding the Sioux Falls area's competitiveness and livability for businesses and individuals.

Dykhouse said the goal of Future Sioux Falls was to bring the community and its leaders together to develop a collective and consistent vision that defines where the community wants to go in a variety of areas including business, education, workforce, culture, and arts and entertainment. The visioning exercise helped Forward Sioux Falls develop action steps for its next program, and on a subconscious level it built cohesiveness among the area's business leaders.

"Subconsciously, that becomes ingrained in the leadership and the direction of Sioux Falls and that's why it's been so important," Dykhouse said. "We publicly go out and say, 'This is what our vision is. This is what we want to see our community like.'"

Sioux Falls during this time period also scored a major victory at the polls that further distanced the city from its anti-growth TACCO days. Back in 1985, Taxpayers Against the Convention Center Obligation blocked construction of a $30 million convention center, performing arts center, and a downtown hotel. Sioux Falls finally approved its performing arts center and convention center/hotel in 1993, but it was missing out on the best concerts and sporting events because of the aging Sioux Falls Arena, a circa-1961 facility built when the city's population was half its current level.

In 2011, a proposed new events center was placed on a special election ballot, and city voters approved the design and construction of the $117 million Denny Sanford PREMIER Center by a 58-percent to 42-percent margin.[2]

The overwhelming support, expressed by voters while the economy was still experiencing adversity from the Great Recession, provided another example of the confidence Forward Sioux Falls has fostered in the community. In addition to the strong and

[2] Harriman, Peter. "Improbable win for events center: Construction to begin next summer." *Argus Leader*, November 9, 2011, accessed July 16, 2020 via Newspapers.com.

FORWARD SIOUX FALLS V — RESULTS ACHIEVED

THE SIOUX EMPIRE HOUSING PARTNERSHIP became the first participant in the mayor's Pettigrew Heights Revitalization Program by constructing five new condominium units.

SHADOW ED coordinated more than 1,650 job shadow experiences.

THE WORKFORCE DEVELOPMENT OFFICE partnered with 38 businesses offering 135 internships and awarded $67,500 in scholarships through the Interns in Industry program.

7,050 JOBS The number of non-farm wage and salaried workers increased by 7,050.

tireless public leadership of Mayor Mike Huether and added support provided by the private sector's Build It Now committee, the Chamber's Young Professionals Network (YPN) played a critical role. YPN's 500-plus members recognized the importance of this game-changing opportunity for the future of Sioux Falls, added energy and enthusiasm to the community conversation, and mobilized a remarkably successful "get out the vote" campaign. YPN's active engagement was essential to securing this landmark quality-of-place project that had been discussed for decades and will provide benefits for generations to come.

"This demonstration of leadership should be viewed as a pivotal point in enhancing the economy and quality of life of the Sioux Falls region, made possible through the support of YPN by Forward Sioux Falls leadership and investors," said Evan Nolte, the Chamber's longtime president and CEO.

SDN Communications CEO Mark Shlanta, in his written message to investors as Forward Sioux Falls V wrapped up its run, expressed confidence that the next program was ready to tackle the challenges raised by NCDS and Future Sioux Falls.

"We're charting a new course, moving toward a brighter future in a whole new world," said Shlanta, who stayed on to co-chair the next program. "The economic realities of the past few years have taught us that we need to be more innovative, more technological, more focused on our targets, and more flexible in our programming."

YPN'S ACTIVE ENGAGEMENT WAS ESSENTIAL TO SECURING THIS LANDMARK QUALITY-OF-PLACE PROJECT.

2006 - 2011

THE GRADUATE EDUCATION AND APPLIED RESEARCH (GEAR) CENTER opened its doors in 2009 and now houses USD's Biomedical Engineering program and three life sciences companies.

$2 BILLION IN CONSTRUCTION Construction values totaled nearly $2 billion from January 2006-December 2010.

$1.06 BILLION Capital investments totaled $1.06 billion from January 2006-December 2010.

CHAPTER 10

Our Time is Now

"FORWARD SIOUX FALLS VI — OUR TIME IS NOW," set out to create 10,000 new jobs while expanding marketing and public relations efforts on a nationwide and global stage. The program also committed to retaining, expanding, and attracting businesses and investing in advocacy, technology, entrepreneurship, and workforce.

Members of the Joint Venture Management Committee settled on a campaign goal of $11.2 million and exceeded fundraising efforts by a million dollars. And once again, the program earned buy-in from businesses of all sizes, said campaign Co-chair Dana Dykhouse.

"People understood that whether they'd be contributing a six-figure contribution or a $500 contribution, they were part of making Sioux Falls better," said Dykhouse. "It's very cliché that a rising tide raises all boats, but that's really the attitude that Sioux Falls has had."

Forward Sioux Falls at this time boasted a record of success, and leaders were confident they were building a trail of momentum. Rather than overhaul its direction, Co-chairs Dykhouse and Shlanta led an effort to refine economic development efforts to:

"IT'S VERY CLICHÉ THAT A RISING TIDE RAISES ALL BOATS, BUT THAT'S REALLY THE ATTITUDE THAT SIOUX FALLS HAS HAD."

- Advocate for the policies, infrastructure, and amenities necessary to ensure Sioux Falls grows effectively and sustainably
- Maximize the economic impact of high-growth businesses, entrepreneurs, and innovators in Sioux Falls through expansion of the South Dakota Technology Business Center, which was rebranded in 2016 as the Zeal Center for Entrepreneurship
- Leverage and expand existing resources to create a skilled workforce pipeline for the area's diverse business sectors and to optimize the resources from Sioux Falls' public and private school systems to two- and four-year degree programs and beyond
- Aggressively promote the Sioux Falls area as a competitive location for business and talent to both external and internal audiences and elevate Sioux Falls' presence in the national market
- Facilitate the expansion of existing public companies and actively target and recruit new businesses to the area, resulting in more jobs, higher income, and an increased tax base

Perhaps the most impactful economic development effort during Forward Sioux Falls VI was born out of an unanticipated business recruitment effort that didn't pan out.

In 2012, an intermediary site selector representing a large Tennessee-based firm reached out to state officials in search of a 400-acre rail-accessible tract of property. The company was looking to build an industrial plant that could employ thousands of workers, and it was clear that Sioux Falls and Rapid City were the only South Dakota cities that could deliver a workforce for such a project, said Pat Costello, then commissioner of the Governor's Office of Economic Development. State officials began working with the Sioux Falls Development Foundation to entice the employer to pick South Dakota.

There was one major problem: Sioux Falls at the time had

no available industrial property anywhere near 400 acres, said Scott Lawrence, who was serving on the Development Foundation board.

"The Development Foundation had 20 acres here, 80 acres here, and we had some good development business, but we did not have a mega-site," said Lawrence, President and CEO of Lawrence & Schiller. "We did not have rail access."

Lawrence, Development Foundation President Slater Barr, and a handful of others traveled to Tennessee to meet with company officials and tour a facility similar to the one being proposed. The company loved Sioux Falls as a potential location, but executives wondered if the city could line up a site of that size and expressed concerns about whether it could deliver on workforce. The Development Foundation team saw the potential of thousands of sustainable high-end jobs and realized that Sioux Falls needed to put together a mega-site regardless if this particular company would become its first tenant.

"Hey, we don't know for sure if these people will come, but we've got to be ready if they ask," Lawrence said. "If it's not them, it's going to be somebody, and we need to be ready."

"IF IT'S NOT THEM, IT'S GOING TO BE SOMEBODY, AND WE NEED TO BE READY."

THE GROUP BEGAN SKETCHING PLANS to acquire land for a mega-site north of Interstate 90 and west of Interstate 29 that would offer convenient access to rail, highways, and redundant energy transmission lines. Development Foundation representatives worked with ag real estate broker Les Miller to secure options from landowners willing to sell property, some of which had been in families for multiple generations. As the company engaged in internal discussions, Sioux Falls business leaders continued working with the site selector and asked BNSF Railway what it would take to build out a Class I rail spur and what federal money would be available.

All was proceeding as planned when Lawrence received the disappointing call from Barr, who had just hung up the phone with the site selector. The company's board, sensing downward economic trends in their industry, decided not to proceed, and the proposed mega-site suddenly had no potential tenant.

The land options were set to expire that summer, and if they did, the state and the Development Foundation surely would never find a similar occasion to assemble such a block of contiguous land, said then South Dakota Governor Dennis Daugaard.

"We really had to jump on that or lose that opportunity forever," Daugaard said.

Daugaard knew he was on board, and he pledged $3 million in grants from the state's Future Fund, which was created in the 1980s to invest in South Dakota's workforce and build its economy. For additional capital, Daugaard and Costello proposed $8.5 million in REDI (Revolving Economic Development and Initiative) Fund loans, an amount that far exceeded any previous REDI financing. The Sioux Falls mega-site endeavor was an even bigger leap of faith for the state, as the fund was being used as a loan vehicle to buy land for which no project was identified.

"No jobs were being created in the near term," Daugaard said. "It was simply to buy vacant land and create the opportunity down the road."

The Board of Economic Development bought into the vision and approved the REDI Fund loans, but those loans would need guarantees. For typical economic development projects, such collateral came in the form of company assets or owners' personal assets. But in this case, there were no companies, no owners—just land with potential future tenants. The Development Foundation reached out to the Forward Sioux Falls VI Joint Venture Management Committee and asked if it could set aside $2.5 million—$500,000 over five years—from the next Forward Sioux Falls initiative to guarantee those notes. Committee members said yes.

That took care of the land, but there would certainly be additional infrastructure costs to prepare the development park for

"WE REALLY HAD TO JUMP ON THAT OR LOSE THAT OPPORTUNITY FOREVER."

potential tenants. And the Development Foundation was in no position to take on those costs, as purchasing so many acres leveraged the organization's current land holdings and hampered its cash flow.

First PREMIER Bank President Dave Rozenboom, who was tapped to co-chair the next Forward Sioux Falls initiative, gathered leaders of the Sioux Falls banking community and asked them to form a coalition to create a $16 million financing package to help provide the needed infrastructure funding. First PREMIER Bank, The First National Bank in Sioux Falls, CorTrust Bank, First Bank & Trust, First Dakota National Bank, Great Western Bank, MetaBank, and U.S. Bank each took a $2 million share in the financing package.

"These people sat down and came together," Lawrence said.

The last piece of the puzzle was a commitment from the City of Sioux Falls. Business leaders convinced Mayor Mike Huether and city councilors that the project could mean more revenue for Sioux Falls than retail development, as retail money turns over in a community one and a half to two times, yet industrial development turns over seven to eight times. City officials agreed, and they committed to help with land annexation, energy utilities, communication access, waste treatment resources, and a new I-90 exit on Marion Road.

On June 2, 2015, atop downtown Sioux Falls' Holiday Inn City Centre, the Development Foundation gathered community members for a celebration to announce Foundation Park, a project more than three years in the making.[1] The 820-acre development park offered a mega-site of up to 390 acres and 117 acres of BNSF Class I rail access.

Lawrence, who by 2015 had moved into the chairmanship role with the Sioux Falls Development Foundation, said the Starlite Room was filled with jubilation and certainly some relief. Some 50 to 75 people put in thousands of hours during the unprecedented three-year collaboration, and the

[1] Schwan, Jodi. "Development Mega-Park Lands Major Project: 820-acre site in northwestern S.F. could employ 8,000." *Argus Leader*, June 3, 2015, accessed July 16, 2020 via Newspapers.com.

Sioux Falls business community came together to take a giant leap of faith.

"The fruit's out on the end of the limb," Lawrence said. "It's a little safer by the trunk, but you've got to go for it sometimes."

Dykhouse said Foundation Park was a leap of faith that needed an influx of "patient capital" with the wherewithal to see the project through years down the road. Forward Sioux Falls, state and city officials, the banks, and donors all worked together to provide that support.

"Everyone came through," Dykhouse said.

"THE FRUIT'S OUT ON THE END OF THE LIMB. IT'S A LITTLE SAFER BY THE TRUNK, BUT YOU'VE GOT TO GO FOR IT SOMETIMES."

During this period, Sioux Falls also made unprecedented progress on some quality-of-life issues raised decades earlier.

The 12,000-seat Denny Sanford PREMIER Center, approved by voters in a 2011 ballot initiative, opened its doors in 2014, attracting an increased selection and variety of world-class concerts such as the Eagles, Paul McCartney, Garth Brooks, James Taylor, Cher, and Paul Simon, and large-scale sporting events that previously had skipped Sioux Falls en route to Omaha and Minneapolis.

Forward Sioux Falls, the Chamber, and the Development Foundation provided $180,000 in local matching funds to help the State of South Dakota purchase land for Good Earth State Park at Blood Run, South Dakota's first new state park in more than 40 years. The picturesque acreage along the Big Sioux River, which features a large oak forest, rolling hills, flood plains, and riverside bluffs, was inhabited by thousands of Oneota Indians into the early 1700s. Land for the park had been pieced together over the years through a partnership between the South Dakota Game, Fish and Parks Department, The Conservation Fund, and the US Forest Service.

June 2012 marked completion of the first phase of the Downtown River Greenway project, improving greenway access and spurring additional private redevelopment along the Big Sioux River.[2] The project turned the east bank into an urban river walk, adding a stepped river edge, a small amphitheater, an

[2] Sneve, Joe. "Greenway sparks $100 million downtown: Celebration marks opening of trail between 6th & 8th." *Argus Leader*, June 9, 2012, accessed July 16, 2020 via Newspapers.com.

informal sitting area, interpretive light piers, a canoe and kayak landing, and a new 200-foot single-span pedestrian bridge. The project also improved bike trail access by adding two ADA-compliant ramps and two new stairways. A second phase completed a year later widened the trail and added seating, river walls, landscaping, and irrigation.

The Sioux Empire Housing Partnership (SEHP), which was created in part to ensure affordable housing opportunities for the growing workforce, launched a website in 2014 geared to the city's growing Hispanic population. The site shared resources to help Spanish-speaking residents achieve the dream of home ownership, offering down-payment assistance and homebuyer education. The partnership reported that in its first 10 years, Forward Sioux Falls' $1 million investment spurred $13 million in economic activity, not including the tax base created by new homeowners.

Forward Sioux Falls VI notched several additional wins for Sioux Falls:

- The program continued partnering with the Sioux Falls Airport Authority to market the Sioux Falls Regional Airport, helping it add flights and new destinations.
- Global marketing and public relations efforts continued, with Sioux Falls earning 1.49 billion impressions in such nationwide outlets as NPR, USA Today, Forbes, Business Week, CNN, CNBC, IndustryWeek, New Geography, U.S. News & World Report, the Chicago Tribune, and Marketplace.
- For business development, Sioux Falls representatives attended 14 national trade shows, participated in 182 conference calls, reached out to 4,324 companies, and held 82 face-to-face meetings. Twenty site selectors visited Sioux Falls, and representatives also spread the city's message at five site selector lunches held in other US cities.

- Through the SDTBC (now Zeal Center for Entrepreneurship), Forward Sioux Falls invested $200,000 in South Dakota Innovation Partners, providing early-stage capital to such start-ups as Medgene Labs, Tranzderm Solutions, and Prairie Aquatech. The center also supported angel investor educational events and the Enterprise Institute's efforts to create new angel funds throughout South Dakota.

The city was blossoming in multiple areas, and more good things loomed in the next Forward Sioux Falls initiative. In his closing note to investors, Shlanta reflected on the program's successes and looked forward to future opportunities.

"Forward Sioux Falls has never been about repeating the same things over and over," Shlanta said. "Throughout each of our six programs, we've reimagined our priorities for our community based on current challenges and opportunities."

FORWARD SIOUX FALLS VI — RESULTS ACHIEVED

NEARLY 11-TO-1 ROI Every dollar invested in Forward Sioux Falls 2011-2016 returned $10.97 in average annual profit for local businesses.

8,421 Total new jobs

$464 MILLION in new personal income

$1.6 BILLION in new business output

$51 MILLION increases in annual tax revenues

63 COMPANIES ASSISTED through business recruitment, retention, and expansion.

2011 - 2016

FOUNDATION PARK is conceptualized and significant efforts to acquire land are initiated

NATIONAL RECOGNITION Successful implementation and marketing elevates the national recognition and viability of the Sioux Falls MSA

COLLABORATED WITH THE SIOUX FALLS AIRPORT AUTHORITY to further enhance air service at the Sioux Falls Regional Airport

BUSINESS RETENTION, ATTRACTION, AND EXPANSION efforts are strategically advanced

CHAPTER 11

Momentum

FOR "FORWARD SIOUX FALLS VII—MOMENTUM," business leaders sought to take the community to an even higher level of success by focusing on people, prosperity, and place. They set a vision to create a dynamic and collaborative environment in which talent, research, and innovative businesses interact to create new ideas, new technologies, and new opportunities impacting not only the region, but also the entire world.

As the greater metropolitan region continued growing well beyond state and national averages, Forward Sioux Falls raised an impressive $15.5 million from investors, $2.5 million of which funded the program's commitment to Foundation Park, and $1.25 million of which helped launch the USD Discovery District. The program also supported workforce attraction, retention, and development; entrepreneurship and innovation; business advocacy and quality-of-place enhancement; and business recruitment, retention, and expansion.

The campaign, co-chaired by First PREMIER Bank President Dave Rozenboom, SDN Communications CEO Mark Shlanta, and Sioux Falls Mayor Mike Huether, committed to:

- Grow the property tax base and add quality jobs through land sales and business attraction, retention, and expansion
- Attract talent and continue to develop the Sioux Falls workforce through creation of education and labor pipelines through workforce training, K-12 and post-secondary education, and utilization of special populations
- Create a superior regional brand that attracts and retains businesses and talent
- Refine governance and operational procedures to realize efficiencies and create best practices

Planning for the program, which launched in 2016, began a year earlier when Forward Sioux Falls continued its collaboration with Atlanta-based Market Street Services to assess Sioux Falls' competitive position and identify education and training strategies to boost workforce sustainability.

The firm helped Forward Sioux Falls develop a Strategic Workforce Action Agenda that identified several key initiatives, including:

- Design and implement a talent marketing campaign, incorporating and coordinating existing efforts along with new strategies
- Develop and optimize a comprehensive online talent portal
- Identify and advance priority programs to support targeted populations in the region
- Develop and implement a cradle-to-career coalition in the Sioux Falls area

As the buildout continued on the city's 820-acre world-class industrial development property, Foundation Park, Sioux Falls business leaders turned their attention to a new university-related research park that was more than a quarter-century in the making.

The idea that evolved into the USD (University of South Dakota) Discovery District originated back in the 1990s with

LEADERS TURNED THEIR ATTENTION TO A NEW UNIVERSITY-RELATED RESEARCH PARK THAT WAS MORE THAN A QUARTER-CENTURY IN THE MAKING.

Governor George Mickelson. Forward Sioux Falls III revived the concept in 2000, embarking on a year-long planning process with more than 200 education, community, and business leaders to sketch out a business incubator and research park. In 2006, the Board of Regents used a gift from the Great Plains Education Foundation to acquire 252 acres to establish a permanent location for University Center Sioux Falls, since rebranded into the USD Community College for Sioux Falls. The 2009 South Dakota Legislature authorized the establishment of an 80-acre research park at the location, and the 2012 Legislature authorized research parks on lands controlled by the South Dakota Board of Regents.

The USD Discovery District is part of a 252-acre site in northwest Sioux Falls that includes two USD Community College for Sioux Falls classroom buildings and the Graduate Education and Applied Research (GEAR) Center. The district provides a setting for students, entrepreneurs, and researchers to interact with each other and foster innovation and economic development.

"The vision for the Discovery District is to create a whole community focused on innovation around the educational components," said Naser, who served as the district's first president.

Leaders expect the USD Discovery District over the next 25 years to grow into a sprawling $314 million complex of 26 buildings, creating 2,800 high-wage research and technology jobs and generating $4.4 million in annual property tax revenues. The venture is a public-private partnership encompassing Forward Sioux Falls, the Chamber, the Development Foundation, the Board of Regents, the University of South Dakota, the Governor's Office of Economic Development, and the City of Sioux Falls. Forward Sioux Falls contributed $500,000 to infrastructure projects for the district and pledged $150,000 annually for operations.

The Board of Regents is providing the land at a lease of just $1 a year for 99 years. Ongoing operations are supported by a four-legged stool, with direct funds coming from USD, the Board of Regents, the City of Sioux Falls, and Forward Sioux Falls. That arrangement is an uncommon way to support a research park, Naser said.

"Usually it's one big player, and a lot of times, it's the state," he said. "So it's a unique funding structure, but it also gets you a lot of people around the table invested in its success."

The USD Discovery District launched with plans for a building to house a research laboratory, office, and biopharmaceutical manufacturing space for SAb Biotherapeutics and Alumend. LifeScape, a nonprofit that serves adults and children with disabilities, announced in January 2020 that it would use 31.6 acres of the district to build a new hospital, school, and rehabilitation center.

"It's all positioned basically to go," Naser said.

> "IT'S PROJECTS LIKE THAT THAT MULTIPLY THEIR EFFECT WITHIN THE LOCAL ECONOMY."

IN OTHER EFFORTS promoting entrepreneurship and innovation, Forward Sioux Falls continued its support of the Zeal Center for Entrepreneurship by setting goals to create 250 new jobs, launch up to 10 new businesses a year through an accelerator challenge, assist 20 companies in securing angel investments, assist 20 companies in securing micro loans, and expand through new satellite locations.

Over the years, Zeal has strengthened and diversified the local economy by helping companies grow and generate jobs with salaries exceeding the regional average, Shlanta said.

"It's projects like that that multiply their effect within the local economy," he said. "To me, those are the things you can point to with Forward Sioux Falls and say 'that was a success.'"

For Foundation Park, which was born out of the previous Forward Sioux Falls effort, the program followed through to provide $500,000 each year for credit enhancement on the state's REDI Fund loans.

In 2018, the development park landed its first anchor tenant, Win Chill Cold Storage, which built out 7.7 million cubic feet of space for blast freezing, freezer, and refrigeration warehousing and distribution.[1] Local trucking company Dakota Carriers followed with an announcement that it would build a 5,600 square-foot office and a 17,500 square-foot mechanical shop in the park, and Nordica Warehouses, Inc. became Foundation Park's third tenant with a 200,000 square-foot facility.

Negotiations to land additional tenants continue.

"Hindsight, in five or six years after the fact, it's been a huge success," said Pat Costello, who helped secure loans for the project when serving as the Governor's Office of Economic Development commissioner. "And in five years in the future when some of these deals that are still in the works start to land, people are going to look at it as that was really a home run for the community and for the state."

And it's just a matter of time before Foundation Park lands its mega-site client. Prior to the development park effort, South Dakota wasn't even in the nationwide conversation to land such big companies, said former Governor Dennis Daugaard, who led South Dakota from 2011 to 2019. The teamwork and commitment that helped make Foundation Park a reality has put Sioux Falls in the game.

"It's already making us players," Daugaard said. "We might not win every time, but we can at least compete."

Forward Sioux Falls didn't let up on the gas in its efforts to attract all kinds of new businesses, initiating meetings with site selectors and national brokers while establishing marketing and business partnerships and national affiliations. It continued advancing regional and national marketing efforts through trade shows, site consultant familiarization tours, drone videos to promote the city's rich park system, and a local brokers partnership program.

"IT'S ALREADY MAKING US PLAYERS. WE MIGHT NOT WIN EVERY TIME, BUT WE CAN AT LEAST COMPETE."

[1] Fugleberg, Jeremy J. "Win Chill set to expand due to high demand." *Argus Leader*, May 1, 2018, accessed July 16, 2020 via Newspapers.com.

Meanwhile, accolades for the city continued pouring in:

- SmartAsset in July 2019 named Sioux Falls the Best City for Young Professionals for the third consecutive year.
- ZipRecruiter in December 2019 named Sioux Falls a top 10 city for jobs.
- *The Wall Street Journal* in February 2020 named Sioux Falls the fifth hottest job market for communities with less than 1 million residents.[2]

Forward Sioux Falls was continuing to show an impressive return on investment. National Community Development Services (NCDS) estimated that every dollar invested in economic development during Forward Sioux Falls VII would return $10.24 in average corporate profits to the community.

Sioux Falls was again reaping the rewards of the business community's forward-thinking efforts, and planning commenced for the next Forward Sioux Falls initiative to launch in 2021.

[2] Oh, Soo. "Austin, Nashville Rank at Top of Hottest U.S. Job Markets." *Wall Street Journal*, February 24, 2020, accessed July 16, 2020, https://www.wsj.com/articles/austin-nashville-rank-at-top-of-hottest-u-s-job-markets-11582545600

FORWARD SIOUX FALLS VII — RESULTS ACHIEVED*

PRIVATE SECTOR RETURN ON INVESTMENT is $4.03 for every $1 invested

7.8% 5-year employment growth

2,714 total new jobs created

$189 MILLION New Annual Personal Income

$2.35 BILLION in non-residential building permits

$274 MILLION new capital investment

*Data reflects only the first four years of this program

2016 - PRESENT

$593 MILLION New Annual Business Output

THE USD DISCOVERY DISTRICT is launched to create an innovation community

FOUNDATION PARK is launched and developed

STRATEGIC WORKFORCE ACTION AGENDA is created to attract, develop, and retain talent

FEDERAL LOBBYING PROGRAM was developed and implemented

CHAPTER 12

The Next Generation of Leaders

OVER ITS 30-PLUS-YEAR HISTORY, Forward Sioux Falls has benefitted from charismatic leaders who thoughtfully considered the needs of their community and turned that insight into a vision for its future. These leaders are creative, collaborative, and capable. They think outside the box and pivot to address new challenges. And their lessons provide a legacy for the next generation of leaders.

On the cusp of the community's eighth economic development program, past and current leaders took a few moments to impart their wisdom on Sioux Falls' up-and-comers. These future leaders honor our Forward Sioux Falls heritage when they engage and get involved in the Sioux Falls way.

The area's successes have been built on trust, risk-taking, strategic partnerships, and leaders' ability to set competitive differences aside in support of overall economic vitality. They welcomed newcomers and invited them to the table. And for the community to continue to thrive and reach the next level, its leaders must continue to adhere to these disciplines.

Tony Bour, who served on the first Forward Sioux Falls board, encourages future leaders to listen well, connect with others,

"SIOUX FALLS DID NOT HAPPEN BY ACCIDENT."

and strive to maintain a positive attitude. Strong leaders will emerge from conversations focused on improving the city.

"Sioux Falls did not happen by accident," Bour said. "Forward Sioux Falls has worked, and it's worked because of the people we've been able to attract."

Fred Slunecka, who worked on Forward Sioux Falls II, III, and IV, agreed that Forward Sioux Falls programs carry an expectation that participants will listen carefully. Put the community first and your own opinions (and your organization's opinions) second. You can make your best persuasive arguments, but pushing your weight around will yield few results, as the Sioux Falls business community doesn't tolerate swagger and bullying, he said.

"Sometimes you just have to leave your guns at the door," said Slunecka, a retired Avera McKennan Hospital CEO. "It's not about you and it's not about your company. It's about what's best for Sioux Falls."

Mark Shlanta, who co-chaired Forward Sioux Falls VI, said much of the city's successes over the years have come from hardworking, dedicated people. He urged those who want to land in leadership positions to be willing to put in the time and hard work.

"If you want to see the city continue to grow and provide opportunities for employers and families, it's going to take effort and vision by you," said Shlanta, CEO of SDN Communications.

Cathy Clark, who co-chaired the fundraising campaign for Forward Sioux Falls IV, said the best leaders she's encountered display an incredible amount of confidence but are able to check their arrogance at the door. That balance is key to gaining respect.

"If you look at lots of different leaders, they're very confident, but the ones who are really good at what they do, they have that arrogance in check," said Clark, retired regional vice president of business banking for Wells Fargo.

Former Governor Dennis Daugaard, who led South Dakota from 2011 to 2019 and helped secure Forward Sioux Falls'

> "IT'S NOT ABOUT YOU AND IT'S NOT ABOUT YOUR COMPANY. IT'S ABOUT WHAT'S BEST FOR SIOUX FALLS."

Foundation Park project, said the lack of ego shown by business leaders and their willingness to collaborate have led to great things for the city of Sioux Falls, which is the state's primary economic driver.

"I think in South Dakota, we're still more intent on accomplishment than attention," he said.

Daugaard said it's also the nature of South Dakota leaders to be a little more frugal and a little more patient.

"We're willing to plant a seedling and be patient while it matures into a beautiful tree," he said. "We don't necessarily have to have a 15-footer transplanted with a tree spade."

Howard Benson, who heads the National Community Development Services (NCDS) firm that consults on Forward Sioux Falls programs, said he's been impressed with the way Sioux Falls business leaders choose cooperation over competitiveness.

"They submerge their corporate interest momentarily in favor of the greater good, knowing that ultimately they would benefit," Benson said. "That is the attitude I've seen in Sioux Falls, and I hope it will continue."

Dana Dykhouse, a campaign co-chair for the sixth and seventh Forward Sioux Falls programs, urges future leaders to get involved and embed themselves into the fabric of the community.

"Don't simply look at your career as trading your time for the company's money," said Dykhouse, president and CEO of First PREMIER Bank. "Don't look at it like that. You have to be more involved. You have to volunteer."

And to the city's veteran business leaders, Dykhouse asks them to seek out someone to mentor and develop into a next-generation leader for Sioux Falls—much like Gary Olson did for him.

"We have shown the way by doing it—not just by saying it, but by doing it," Dykhouse said.

Pam Hanneman, who led small- to medium-sized business fundraising efforts during the first Forward Sioux Falls initiative,

> "WE HAVE SHOWN THE WAY BY DOING IT—NOT JUST BY SAYING IT, BUT BY DOING IT"

said you can recognize strong leadership in people's energy, words, body language, and their willingness to go out and do things themselves. She said the most successful leaders she's encountered over her career don't just give orders; they practice what they preach.

"They were in the trenches," said Hanneman, vice president of business banking for First PREMIER Bank. "That's what I like to see—people in the trenches doing it themselves."

Steve Kirby, a Bluestem Capital Company founding partner who worked on Forward Sioux Falls III and IV, said future leaders should develop a hunch as to what the community should look like 5 or 10 years from now, bring their vision to it, and get involved. They should be humble, self-sacrificing, and willing to go out and do what they say they'll do.

And for current leaders looking to elevate the next generation, they should put a priority on succession and grooming. Leadership doesn't just happen; those skills need to be developed so today's leaders can ensure future success.

"They want to pass the baton to qualified people," Kirby said.

First PREMIER Bank President Dave Rozenboom, who co-chaired Forward Sioux Falls VII and chaired the JVMC, said it's important to recognize the inevitable ebbs and flows in the economy, yet economic development efforts must continue in both.

"When times are good, it's easy to say we don't need to. When times are bad, it's easy to say we can't," Rozenboom said. "In all circumstances, we find a way to invest in our community. This is how we set Sioux Falls apart."

Evan Nolte, who led the Sioux Falls Area Chamber of Commerce for decades, said inclusion and collaboration are extremely important leadership traits, and personal relationships are powerful. You can be the smartest person in the world, but if your attitude is "it's only me," you're going to have difficulty making a difference. Join in, he said.

"You shouldn't sit there and wait to be called," Nolte said. "You have talent. You need to get involved with other people."

"THEY WANTED TO MOVE SIOUX FALLS FORWARD, AND THEY DID."

Lyle Schroeder, the longtime Sioux Valley Hospital president, said the business leaders he worked alongside on the first Forward Sioux Falls campaign demonstrated a tremendous work ethic, brought a successful attitude from their own companies, and displayed a willingness to become team players for community activities. They were the "cream of the crop" and exuded love for their city.

"They wanted to move Sioux Falls forward, and they did," Schroeder said.

To the numerous business leaders reading this book who have played a part in Forward Sioux Falls' success, thank you. You have put your community ahead of yourself and your business to help your city achieve greatness. And if you look around, you'll find a younger version of yourself who can do the same. Maybe that person looks like you, and maybe they don't. But you will recognize them for their passion, drive, and commitment to our community. Identify that up-and-coming leader to mentor and invite them to participate in the process.

STEP FORWARD AND JOIN IN.

To the emerging leaders who want to be part of this success, join in and do it today. Put your talents to work for a higher purpose and help the city continue its extraordinary march forward. You'll find the effort rewarding, and in 10, 20, or 30 years, after you've completed your term as a campaign chair or other significant leadership role, you can keep the momentum going by finding that next-generation leader to mentor.

Sioux Falls' success can be attributed to selfless leaders collaborating to advance common goals. Every five years, they reengage as part of an intentional process packed with vision and accountability to push the city forward. That's Forward Sioux Falls.

Step forward and join in.

About Forward Sioux Falls

ESTABLISHED IN 1987 as a joint venture between the Sioux Falls Area Chamber of Commerce (now Greater Sioux Falls Chamber of Commerce) and the Sioux Falls Development Foundation, Forward Sioux Falls is the premier economic driver for the Sioux Falls region. Possessing a mantra of "A rising tide lifts all boats," Forward Sioux Falls serves as the programmatic conduit for multiple economic and workforce development initiatives.

Every five years, Forward Sioux Falls engages the business community to formulate a freshly-imagined program of work. This design is accomplished through a series of interviews, and feedback is combined with metric-driven data so that the objectives remain laser-focused and the outcomes meet or exceed expectations. Much of this work is accomplished through the Development Foundation and Chamber; however, partnerships are also leveraged to elevate projects, some of which will ultimately become self-sustaining.

Sioux Falls area businesses understand the importance of working together, which is demonstrated by how competitors put their differences aside for the collective benefit of a unified community. The result of this resolve has been the significant return on investment that the public and private sector have experienced over the past three plus decades.

As the programmatic funding mechanism for vital workforce and economic development initiatives, Forward Sioux Falls provides opportunities that positively affect our people, prosperity, and place. These efforts continue to be affirmed on a national scale with accolades including, but not limited to Sioux Falls being named among the best places to live, secure a job, start a business, and retire.